Cambridge Elements ≡

Elements in the Philosophy of Science
edited by
Jacob Stegenga
University of Cambridge

SCIENTIFIC MODELS AND DECISION-MAKING

Eric Winsberg
*University of Cambridge
and University of South Florida*

Stephanie Harvard
The University of British Columbia

CAMBRIDGE
UNIVERSITY PRESS

Shaftesbury Road, Cambridge CB2 8EA, United Kingdom

One Liberty Plaza, 20th Floor, New York, NY 10006, USA

477 Williamstown Road, Port Melbourne, VIC 3207, Australia

314–321, 3rd Floor, Plot 3, Splendor Forum, Jasola District Centre,
New Delhi – 110025, India

103 Penang Road, #05–06/07, Visioncrest Commercial, Singapore 238467

Cambridge University Press is part of Cambridge University Press & Assessment,
a department of the University of Cambridge.

We share the University's mission to contribute to society through the pursuit of
education, learning and research at the highest international levels of excellence.

www.cambridge.org
Information on this title: www.cambridge.org/9781009468213

DOI: 10.1017/9781009029346

First published 2024

A catalogue record for this publication is available from the British Library.

ISBN 978-1-009-46821-3 Hardback
ISBN 978-1-009-01432-8 Paperback
ISSN 2517-7273 (online)
ISSN 2517-7265 (print)

Scientific Models and Decision Making

Elements in the Philosophy of Science

DOI: 10.1017/9781009029346
First published online: January 2024

Eric Winsberg
University of Cambridge and University of South Florida

Stephanie Harvard
The University of British Columbia

Author for correspondence: Eric Winsberg, winsberg@usf.edu

Abstract: This Element introduces the philosophical literature on models, with an emphasis on normative considerations relevant to models for decision-making. Section 1 gives an overview of core questions in the philosophy of modelling. Section 2 examines the concept of model adequacy for purpose, using three examples of models from the atmospheric sciences to describe how this sort of adequacy is determined in practice. Section 3 explores the significance of using models that are not adequate for purpose, including the purpose of informing public decisions. Section 4 provides a basic framework for values in modelling, using a case study to highlight the ethical challenges when building models for decision-making. The Element concludes by establishing the need for strategies to manage value judgements in modelling, including the potential for public participation in the process.

Keywords: models, climate, decision-making, Covid-19, philosophy

ISBNs: 9781009468213 (HB), 9781009014328 (PB), 9781009029346 (OC)
ISSNs: 2517-7273 (online), 2517-7265 (print)

Contents

1 Introduction

1.1 What Is a Model?

If there is anything that could be described as a core question in the philosophy of modelling in science, it is probably *What is a model*? Unfortunately, this question is deceptively complex: as we will see, it is tangled up with numerous other key questions in this branch of philosophy. But since we have to start somewhere, let's give it a shot: what *is* a model? Here's a short list of examples of things scientists call models:

(1) A 'typical' drawing of a cell in a biology textbook, showing the cell to contain a nucleus, a cell membrane, a Golgi body, mitochondria, and endoplasmic reticulum (Downes 1992) (Figure 1).

(2) The standard laboratory rat, *Rattus norvegicus*, depicted in Figure 2, is a model organism which is studied with the goal of understanding a range of biological phenomena, including humans (Ankeny and Leonelli 2021, chap. 2; Leonelli 2010; Levy and Currie 2015).

(3) The solar system, used by Niels Bohr in the early twentieth century as a model of the atom. Bohr argued that the nucleus of an atom is like the Sun, the electrons like planets circling the Sun (Giere, Bickle, and Mauldin 1979).

(4) The Friedmann–Lemaître–Robertson–Walker models of cosmology and the standard model of particle physics. The former is a way of picking out a particular set of conditions that satisfies the equations of the theory of general relativity; the latter a means of fleshing out the mathematical framework provided by quantum field theory (Redhead 1980; Smeenk 2020). This idea of a scientific model bearing the relation to theory that a model bears to a set of axioms in logic goes back to Mary Hesse (1967).

(5) Watson and Crick's famous double-helix models, built from pieces of wire and tin plates (depicted in Figure 3) and ultimately taken to represent the structure of DNA (Giere, Bickle, and Mauldin 1979, 16–29).

(6) A model reconstruction of the Earth's temperature in past geological periods, developed using proxy data from sources like deep ice cores, fossilized shells, tree rings, corals, lake sediments, and boreholes (Parker 2018; Winsberg 2018, chap. 2). An example of this is depicted in Figure 4.

(7) The San Francisco Bay model, depicted in Figure 5 – made of concrete, replete with pumps, and filled with salt water when in operation – used to simulate the behaviour of water in the real San Francisco Bay. The Army Corps of Engineers constructed the model in the 1950s to predict the effects of a proposal to close off the Golden Gate and turn the Bay into a freshwater reservoir (Weisberg 2013).

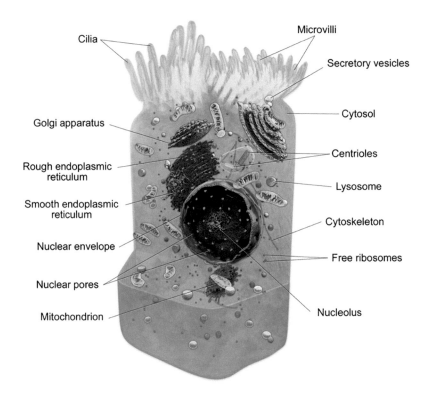

Anatomy of a Cell

Figure 1 A model of a plant cell.

Source: www.pinterest.ca/pin/plant-cell-vs-animal-cell-whats-the-difference–533746993338085307/.

Figure 2 A model organism, the white lab rat.

Source: Williams (2011).

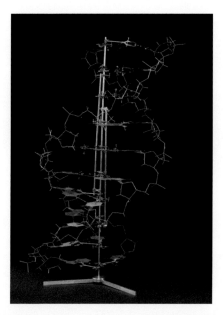

Figure 3 Watson and Crick's tin plate model.

Source: https://collection.sciencemuseumgroup.org.uk/objects/co146411/crick-and-watsons-dna-molecular-model-molecular-model.

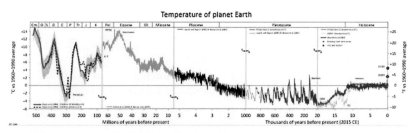

Figure 4 Several different models of the Earth's paleoclimate, presented as one history.

Source: Glen Fergus, CC BY-SA 3.0, https://commons.wikimedia.org/w/index.php?curid=31736468.

(8) Weather and climate models that run on computers (an example is depicted in Figure 6), which are used to make *predictions* about actual short-term weather conditions and *projections* about possible long-term climate conditions under different CO_2 emissions scenarios (Parker 2018; Winsberg 2018).

(9) Epidemiological models that forecast or explain the spread of an infectious disease (Winsberg and Harvard 2022). An example is shown in Figure 7.

Figure 5 The San Francisco Bay model.
Source: https://commons.wikimedia.org/w/index.php?curid=30086231.

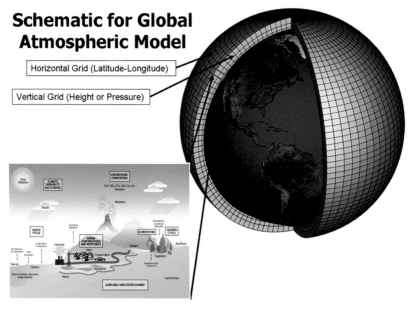

Figure 6 A global climate model.
Source: www.gfdl.noaa.gov/climate-modeling/.

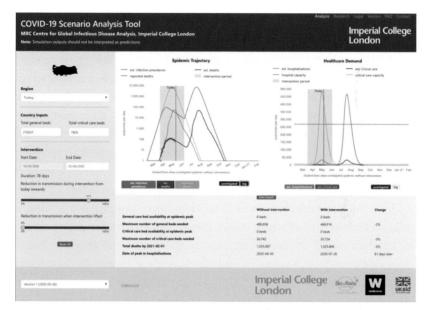

Figure 7 A model run of the Imperial College London Covid-19 model 'Covidsim'.

Source: https://covidsim.org.

(10) Health-economic decision models, which compare the costs and consequences of implementing different healthcare programmes, interventions, or technologies (Briggs, Sculpher, and Claxton 2006).

One thing that is noticeable about this list is that it is extremely heterogeneous. Take, to begin with, the standard models of cosmology and particle physics: while they are very commonly called models, they are really complements to physical *theories*. Compare these to climate models and epidemiological models: although the construction of these models is in part *guided by theory*, they are more like stand-alone bits of *mathematics*. With regard to the San Francisco Bay model and Watson and Crick's double-helix models, these are *actual physical entities*, which were *built* by humans for scientific purposes. The standard laboratory rat is a variety of a biological species *bred* by humans for these purposes, while the solar system is a *found object* that Bohr used to articulate his conception of what the atom looked like. And, unlike these physical entities, a reconstructed record of the Earth's temperature in a past geological period is a *data model* (Bailer-Jones 2009; Bokulich 2011; Hartmann 1995; Laymon 1982; Leonelli 2016, 2019; Mayo 1996, 2018; Suppes 1962, 2007): 'a corrected, rectified, regimented, and in many instances idealized version of the data we gain from immediate observation, the so-called raw data' (Frigg and Hartmann 2012).

In fact, our short, yet extremely heterogeneous list of models reflects a key source of confusion about models: *there is very little one can say about scientific models that will be generally true of all of them.* In this Element, instead of trying to work our way through this confusion, our plan is to live with it, so we can focus on other issues. In this section, we will simply zero in on a few features that *many* models have, so we can later explore how those features are important for understanding philosophical issues that arise in connection with certain models – especially those that play a role in helping policy-makers to craft policies that affect us all.

There is one more source of confusion that we must address before we move on. This is the rather haphazard way in which ordinary language use in science invokes a famous triad of terms: *model, theory,* and *experiment.* As we noted, the 'standard model of particle physics' is really a part of theory – but is a theory different from a model? This is far from clear, especially since when we talk about our best *theories* of how diseases spread or of how turbulence arises, what we are really talking about are things that involve *modelling.* Furthermore, there is an influential line of thought in philosophy of science that asserts that theories are nothing more than families of models (Suppes 1960; Suppe 1972; van Fraassen 1980). Nancy Cartwright (1983, 1989) argues that theories are incomplete without accompanying models – models are involved whenever a mathematical theory is applied to the real world. Finally, experiments are often described as being carried out under a 'model' of what the experimental system is and how it is manipulated in the laboratory (Suppes 1969).

In light of this, how can we possibly distinguish between a theory, a model, and an experiment? In fact, attempting to draw the line between these has been a central activity in the philosophy of modelling for many decades. For the purpose of this Element, however, it will suffice to employ a very simple distinction between theory, model, and experiment. Here, we take the word 'theory' to mean a particularly well-supported, widely-respected, and successful – in other words, *well-credentialled* – way of understanding how the world works (we will set aside the question of whether such an entity comprises a family of models, a syntactic structure, or whatever else (Suppe 1972)). In comparison, models and experiments can be more or less well-credentialled; that is, neither term flags a particular level of epistemic support or record of success. With regard to the difference between models and experiments, we will not draw any particular distinction in this Element: we simply use the word 'modelling' to convey a scientific process carried out either with paper and pencil or on a computer, and the word 'experiment' to convey a scientific process, the canonical form of which takes place in a laboratory by poking and prodding at a sample of the kind of system that is of interest.

With that said, let's begin by zeroing in on three features that many models have. First, models are almost always integrated into a *triad*. In other words, when we talk about modelling, we are almost always referring to three things: (1) a system or other phenomenon in the world, which we call the *target*; (2) the model itself, which *represents* the target (more on this shortly); and (3) the model *user*. These three things must be understood in relation to each other: in particular, the model user cannot be ignored because it is her *intentions* that ultimately determine the model's target system and the model's purpose. In other words, models are only representations of their target systems because a model user says they are. For example, the solar system has been around for billions of years – but it only became a model that represents the target system 'the atom' when a human agent, Niels Bohr, singled it out and said 'that's a model of the atom'. Similarly, a particular computer model has the cognitive function of predicting the weather tomorrow rather than of projecting the climate at the end of the century because its user says so. Indeed, a model only has a cognitive function at all, rather than the function of being a video installation in an art museum, because its user says so.

Second, as noted, models are almost always *representations* of target systems. What exactly it means for something to be a scientific representation is another core area of inquiry in philosophy of modelling, with a rich literature that we will not review here (Frigg and Nguyen 2021). For our purposes, it will suffice to say that a model *represents* a target system if a model user takes it to stand for that target system in a way that helps the model user reason about that system (Morgan and Morrison 1999; Morrison 1999); R. I. G. Hughes' (1997) 'Denotation–Demonstration–Interpretation' account of modelling is especially useful here. Some have even argued that there is a kind of use of models along these lines that gives rise to its own style of 'model-based reasoning' (Magnani, Nersessian, and Thagard 1999; Knuuttila 2005, 2011; Magnani and Nersessian 2002; Peschard 2011) in which 'inferences are made by means of creating models and manipulating, adapting and evaluating them' (Nersessian 2010, quoted in Frigg and Hartmann 2012).

Furthermore, because models are representations of target systems – not perfectly complete and entirely accurate depictions of those systems – the modelling process involves pragmatic choices about what to represent and how to represent it, which we call *representational decisions* (Harvard and Winsberg 2022). A well-worn analogy is useful at this point: models are like maps. Think about a subway map: the choices that go into how to represent the world in a subway map have a great deal to do with how the map will be used. The purpose of a subway map is to help people figure out how to get from station A to station B ('Is there a single line that takes me there? Am I going to have to make changes along the way?'). So, a subway map is designed to represent the features of the world that are salient to being able to decide how to get from point A to point B. Subway map users don't particularly care how far the different stops are from each other, nor do they care if the path between two stops is a straight line or if the subway takes a curved path to get somewhere. The key to making a good subway map is carefully choosing the most useful information to represent and using representational conventions that, together, make it as easy as possible for users to reason about and identify the best way to get from A to B.

Models are a lot like this. Like maps, they are things that we build to represent the world and to help us reason about it. And they reflect *choices* about how to represent the world: model developers decide 'we're going to include this, we're *not* going to include that'. Think of Watson and Crick's tin plate and wire model of DNA. It was very important for them to represent, in their model, the length of the four nitrogen-containing nucleobases (cytosine (C), guanine (G), adenine (A), and thymine (T)), but not their internal molecular structure. That is because they were trying to reason about how these four nucleobases could fit together like a puzzle. So they used a (3D) puzzle-piece–like representational toolkit to build the model and to help them do that reasoning.

This brings us to our third extremely important feature of many models. Their criterion of adequacy is most often not that they are 'true' to the world. It is not an important criticism of a subway map that the Broadway line 'isn't really orange', or that the map doesn't show that some subway lines cross bodies of water by going under them in tunnels while others go over them on bridges. Yet it *would* be an important criticism of a subway map if it were to represent two nearby stations by the exact same dot on the map. After all, this would make users think they could change lines at that stop without leaving the system, and avoiding this kind of mistake is what subway maps are supposed to facilitate. Part of a subway map's intended purpose is to help users make accurate inferences about where and how to change subway lines. With models, as with maps, the criterion of adequacy is that they are good enough for the purposes we intend to use them for. Sometimes meeting certain purposes requires that the representational relationship between the model (or map) and the world is verisimilitude. But often it does not. And adequacy for purpose is the telos of a model and a map, not truth.

Whether or not this fact about models, along with the fact that models very often involve deliberate distortions, poses a threat to scientific realism is a topic of much philosophical debate. The threat might arise (according to the debate) if one assumes, as many philosophers do, that science is fundamentally a model-based activity (most famously Nancy Cartwright (Cartwright 1983, 1989, 2019), Ronald Giere (Giere 1988, 1999, 2006; Giere, Bickle, and Mauldin 1979), and Margaret Morrison (Morgan and Morrison 1999; Morrison 1999, 2000, 2005, 2009)).[1]

1.2 Are There 'Types' of Models?

Given all of the above, it is not surprising that philosophers have made various attempts to classify models into *types*. Some of these classification attempts have corresponded to key questions like 'How does the model represent?' and 'What is the model's cognitive function?'. Partly because it is a closely related question, and partly because philosophers are always fascinated by ontological questions, the question 'What kind of entity is a model?' often also plays a central role in classifications of models. We will not explore here all the philosophical attempts to classify models (see, especially, Frigg and Hartmann (2012) and Weisberg (2013) if this is of interest). However, the following rough division of models into four categories will be helpful in tying together some of the central issues that concern us in this Element. We should emphasize that not everyone will find this categorization scheme adequate, especially readers who are concerned with understanding the most heterogeneous lists of models.

1.2.1 Abstract/Mental Models

Consider our very first example of something scientists call a model: a picture of a cell in a biology textbook. This what Stephen Downes (1992) has called an 'idealized' exemplar. As Downes notes, textbooks will present a schematized cell that contains items of interest: in a botany textbook the schematized cell will contain chloroplasts and an outer cell wall, but in a zoology textbook the schematized cell will not include those things (1992, 145). As Downes puts it, 'the cell is a model in a large group of interrelated models that enable us to understand the operations of all cells. The model is not a nerve cell, nor is it a muscle cell, nor a pancreatic cell, it stands for all of these' (1992, 145). As we will see, abstract/mental models have much in common with our next category

---

[1] For a discussion of whether a fundamentally model-based conception of science is compatible with scientific realism, see section 5.1 of Frigg and Hartmann (2012) and references therein, especially Hartmann (1998); Laymon (1985); Massimi (2018a, 2018b); Morrison (2000); Saatsi (2016); and Teller (2018).

of models, *concrete models*. However, one important difference should be emphasized. Making inferences from abstract/mental models requires model users to have an implicit understanding of the target system that allows them to do something akin to mentally simulating its behaviour. Unlike the concrete models we describe next, abstract/mental models, like a simple drawing of a cell, *do not mechanically generate their own behaviour.*

1.2.2 Concrete Models

Some examples of concrete models from our introductory list are the San Francisco Bay model, the solar system as a model of the atom, and the laboratory rat as a model of biological phenomena in humans. What seems to be special about concrete models is that they come with their own dynamical behaviour *and* they represent and support dynamical inferences by purporting to be a causal duplicate of the target system. For example, the San Francisco Bay model is a concrete thing that mechanically generates its own behaviour: water literally sloshes in the model, and when it sloshes in a particular way in the model, the user infers that water will slosh similarly in the real San Francisco Bay. While concrete models are not the only type of model that is meant to license dynamical inferences about their target systems, they are the only type of model that does this by presenting actual behaviour. As a result of this built-in behaviour, users of a concrete model do not need to know how to reason about how the system should be expected to evolve – rather, a concrete model demonstrates that evolution. For example, a schematized cell in a biology textbook (an abstract/mental model) does not demonstrate to us how mitochondria behave in cells, but a laboratory rat (a concrete model) might very well be used to demonstrate this behaviour.

When considering concrete models, a sometimes useful distinction is that between analogical models (Bailer-Jones 2002, 2009; Bailer-Jones and Bailer-Jones 2002; Hesse 1963, 1967, 1974) and scale models (Black 1962; Sterrett 2006, 2021). Both analogical models and scale models are concrete, but an analogical model is found (e.g., the solar system as a model of the atom) and a scale model is constructed (e.g., the San Francisco Bay model). While inferences from model to target are probably the most straightforward in the case of scale models, this does not necessarily translate into reliability. It is very easy to see what the San Francisco Bay model says about what will happen in the real San Francisco Bay. However, the inference is only as reliable as the assumption that one is a causal duplicate of the other. In fact, this is almost certainly not true in this case, because fluids have scale-dependent features. The San Francisco Bay model was mostly used for rhetorical purposes (more on the use of models for rhetorical purposes in Section 3).

1.2.3 Data Models

An example of a data model from our introductory list is a reconstructed record of the Earth's temperature in past geological periods that is developed using proxy data. A data model is essentially a summary of information – a *corrected, normalized, systematized,* and *idealized* summary – that scientists believe is relevant to their reconstruction project and that they have collected from various data sources. For example, scientists may start by summarizing variations in the ratio of different isotopes of oxygen in deep ice cores and in the fossilized shells of tiny animals (Parker 2018) and gradually incorporate this data model into another to draw inferences about the Earth's temperature in the past. Examples of other familiar data models come from randomized controlled trials and observational studies in the health sciences: for example, when a new drug is developed, researchers will routinely collect selected pieces of information from people who are taking and those who are not taking the drug and summarize it in the form of a data model (e.g., descriptive statistical models of clinical outcomes). Such data models often become useful sources of clinical information that are perceived to be relevant to and can be incorporated into other research projects, including computational models (described in the next subsection). For example, a randomized controlled trial may find that patients who receive a new asthma drug have an annual rate of asthma exacerbation of 0.11 (95% CI 0.10, 0.13), while patients who receive an existing asthma drug have an annual rate of exacerbation of 0.12 (95% CI 0.10, 0.14). This summary of clinical information may then be incorporated as a *parameter* in the sort of model that is used to explore the cost-effectiveness of a new medication (e.g., FitzGerald et al. 2020). Importantly, data models also play a central role in evaluating computational models. That is, the results of computational models will often be directly compared to data models as a means of assessing whether their results are consistent with our existing knowledge about the world. Although our focus in the later sections of this Element is not on data models themselves, they are a key component of the models we focus on. In this context, the important thing to keep in mind is that data and data models 'are representations that are products of a process of inquiry' (Bokulich and Parker 2021, 31). Like the other models we discuss, data models involve representational choices, and our objective is for them to be *adequate for purpose*, not true or false.

1.2.4 Mathematical (including Computational) Models

At a high level, the purpose of mathematical models is to be able to fit together mathematical relationships that we think describe the world and apply them to a target system. Those mathematical relationships can be bits of theory, law, mathematical regularity, rules of behaviour, or the product of our own human reasoning. We then use the mathematical model to reason about that target system and help us better understand it. Think of a weather system, a hurricane, traffic patterns, predator–prey relations in an ecosystem, or the spread of disease in a human population. In a weather model, we fit together laws of thermodynamics with laws that govern the dynamical flow of parcels of air in the atmosphere. In a hurricane model, we treat the atmosphere as a fluid that we divide into parcels and use basic primitive laws of motion as well as thermodynamic laws of gas dynamics to calculate how those parcels of air will move around. In a traffic model, we give each car (with its driver) a set of rules for when it will speed up, slow down, or stop depending on what it sees in its environment. In a predator–prey model, we fit together our best assumptions about the rate at which predators kill prey with the rate at which predators die when they fail to capture prey. At the end of the day, the goal is to integrate various salient bits of theory and other mathematical regularities that we have some trust in so that they can be applied to draw out inferences about the *target system* (the hurricane or the traffic jam) by reasoning with the model (Morgan and Morrison 1999, chap. 1; Winsberg 2010).

Computational models can be understood as a subset of mathematical models. A mathematical model becomes computational when the bits of math in the model become too analytically intractable to draw the needed inferences using pencil and paper. Often this is because the model involves differential equations that can't be solved analytically (Winsberg 2010). But it can also be because the mathematical model is more about rules of behaviour than it is about solvable or unsolvable equations.

Earlier we pointed out that abstract/mental models are quite different from concrete models in that the latter mechanically generate their own behaviour while the former require model users to effectively mentally simulate the behaviour of the target system. As a result, what behaviour abstract/mental models will predict depends quite a bit on what the model user brings to the task. Mathematical models, interestingly, straddle this divide. If you have a basic pencil and paper model with which you can make simple calculations, then the model just does what it does, not unlike a concrete model. However, if the mathematical model needs to be turned into a computational model, then how that gets implemented by its builder/user will often have a significant effect on what behaviour it exhibits.

1.3 Mathematical and Computational Models: A Closer Look

In this subsection, we delve in greater detail into mathematical and computational models; Sections 2, 3, and 4 will focus on philosophical issues connected specifically with these models. Our main goal in this subsection is to establish that mathematical models can vary along at least five overlapping continua – *idealization, articulation, credentials, sensitivity,* and *skill* –and to explain how we will use these terms in the remainder of this Element.

1.3.1 Idealization

It has become popular in recent philosophy of science to call certain kinds of models 'idealized' models, and to divide so-called idealization into 'Aristotelian idealization' (McMullin 1985) and 'Galilean idealization' (Cartwright 1989). On this account, Aristotelian idealization consists of 'stripping away', in our imagination, all properties from a concrete object that we believe are not relevant to the problem at hand. This allows us to focus on a limited set of properties in isolation. An example is a classical mechanics model of the planetary system, which describes the planets as objects only having shape and mass and disregards all other properties. Galilean idealizations, on the other hand, are ones that involve deliberate *distortions*. Physicists build models consisting of point masses moving on frictionless planes, economists assume that agents are omniscient, biologists study isolated populations, and so on. It was characteristic of Galileo's approach to science to use simplifications of this sort whenever a situation was too complicated to tackle (Frigg and Hartmann 2012). In mathematical models, Aristotelian and Galilean idealization usually work in harmony. Indeed, the two generally go hand in hand for good reason: so-called Galilean idealization usually only works insofar as some degree of 'Aristotelian' reasoning is in play. If we do too much Galilean idealization without ensuring that this idealization doesn't affect what is 'relevant' to us, we will get into trouble. Making the two kinds of idealization work in harmony is part of the way we ensure that our models are adequate for purpose. The takeaway point is that mathematical models (including computational models) can vary in terms of how idealized they are, both in terms of the degree to which they simplify reality (i.e., exclude elements of the target system from the representation) and distort it (i.e., deliberately change elements of the target system in the representation).

1.3.2 Articulation

Earlier, we drew attention to the fact that mathematical models seem to come in two varieties. Sometimes, a mathematical model invites us to use simple paper and pencil methods to draw out inferences about the world. Other times, a mathematical model needs to be augmented with additional reasoning, including reasoning about which computational methods can and will be used to implement it – and, as we said, how a computational model gets implemented will often have a significant effect on what behaviour it exhibits. Consider the case of a computational model designed to simulate fluid flows that contain significant shock discontinuities. The existence of shocks makes it difficult to turn the differential equations of fluid dynamics into a step-by-step algorithm that a computer can calculate without errors compounding and blowing up. A host of different strategies, including the so-called piecewise parabolic method discussed in Winsberg (2010, 46), is an extreme case of a mathematical model needing substantial augmentation in order to be implemented successfully, and different implementations could lead to substantially different results. A useful piece of vocabulary to help understand the degree to which a mathematical model needs to be supplemented with additional reasoning in order to successfully calculate with it is *articulation*. We can say that the simplest paper and pencil model will not require any articulation at all, while any computational model will require at least some degree of articulation; the more complex the computational model, the more articulation it will require. A model comprising differential equations of fluid dynamics that we hope will enable us to calculate the behaviour of shocks will require enormous articulation. Only a model that requires no articulation will just 'do what it does', that is, generate its own behaviour like a concrete model (see Section 2.4). Note that it may be tempting to say that once we have finished developing a computational model, the model just 'does what it does'. However, this is only really true if we zero in on a specific version of the model, written with a specific set of instructions, run on a specific piece of hardware, and compiled by a specific compiler. Otherwise, the 'same' computational model (if it is complex enough) can very easily exhibit substantially different behaviour. It is therefore very useful to understand mathematical and computational models with reference to the degree of articulation they require.

1.3.3 Sensitivity

In many contexts, a model's *sensitivity* refers to how sensitive its output is to choices of parameter values. More generally, it could refer to how sensitive the model's output is to methodological choices of any kind. It is important to distinguish a model's sensitivity to choices of parameter values and the sensitivity that the system it models exhibits to the initial value of its variables. Here we are concerned with the former.

What is the difference between a variable and a parameter? A parameter value is the value of some measurable quantity associated with the system that stays fixed throughout the life of the system over the timescale of the model, while a variable, obviously, varies. A variable for a model is thus both an input for a model (the value the variable takes at an initial time) and an output (the value the variable takes at all subsequent times – including, of course, at the final time of a model run). A parameter is simply an input. So, for example, in an epidemiological model, it might be that the reproductive rate of the virus is a parameter, and the value for the number of people infected at any one time is a variable.

When building mathematical models, there can be varying levels of uncertainty about what to represent in the model and how to represent it. In some cases, there is a wealth of well-established background knowledge about the target system, which functions to inform and even *constrain* representational decisions. For example, when modellers build computational models of the motions of the planets in the solar system, modellers' representational decisions are constrained by the well-established laws of celestial mechanics. However, in other cases, background knowledge about a target system is lacking: there is far more uncertainty around what should be represented in the model and how. In these cases, we say that representational decisions are *unconstrained*. When a model is built under these conditions, it is important for modellers to explore whether and how model results change when they make different representational decisions. In other words, it is important to explore how *sensitive* model results are to changes in representational decisions. If the value of X that a model calculates is highly sensitive to representational decisions, and those decisions are not highly constrained, we have reasons not to trust the model to give us precise predictions of the value of X.

1.3.4 Credentials

Roughly speaking, a model's credentials correspond to how much trust we should put in it: the degree to which we should expect the model not to let us down, but rather to prove to be a successful way of understanding how the world works. In the case of mathematical models, model credentials are intrinsically linked to the *ancestries* of whatever bits of math have gone into making them. After all, bits of math can come from almost any source we use to gain knowledge about the world: they can come from theory, from patterns we see in data that we think are robust, or just basic assumptions we think are plausible (for whatever reason). If the bits of math that go into a model come from theory, this will help to give the model credentials (as we described in Section 1.1, we reserve the term 'theory' for a *well-credentialled* way of understanding the world, one that enjoys not only wide recognition but a history of success). If the bits of math that go into making a mathematical model come, not from theory but from *models of data*, then those bits of math will only be as good and as widely applicable as those models of data – the model's credentials are linked to the data models. And if those bits of math come not from theory, not from data models, but from human intuitions of what is plausible, then those bits of math will only be as reliable as human intuitions are. A model whose credentials are intrinsically linked to human intuitions is one we should put less trust in.

To give an example, imagine we are building a climate model and we need a bit of math that calculates how much infrared radiation the Earth radiates back as it absorbs ultraviolet radiation from the Sun. To find one, we can reach for the Stefan–Boltzmann law, which is a direct application of Planck's law, which is ultimately grounded in the well-established theory of quantum mechanics. Putting a mathematical relationship like that into our climate model is unlikely to let us down. On the other hand, imagine we need a bit of math that calculates how many clouds and of what kind will form in various parcels of the atmosphere. Unfortunately, it is unlikely that we will be able use basic physics to calculate this: in general, climate models are too coarse-grained to 'resolve' cloud formation (Winsberg 2010, 2018). Instead, we will need to come up with a *subgrid model* of cloud formation. The goal of a subgrid model is to dictate a function that will tell us how much cloud structure there is in each grid cell of the simulation as a function of the temperature, humidity, pressure, and other variables in the grid cell. Because subgrid models often require a number of parameter values to specify them, they are often called *parameterizations*. These subgrid models have complex ancestries: they are derived from laboratory experiment, field observation, and, more recently, from the output of machine learning algorithms. None of these sources will have the same credentials as our piece of math that calculates infrared radiation. Furthermore, it is not uncommon in climate models for the parameterization of cloud formation to be deliberately wrong – so as to offset other errors that climate models are known to have (Mauritsen et al. 2012). This highlights an important fact about representational decisions: the best representational decision is the one that is most adequate for purpose, not necessarily the one that is true to the world. The 'best' parameterization of cloud formation in a climate model might not be the one that most accurately depicts cloud formation, but the one that, in conjunction with all the other representational decisions, makes the model most adequate for purpose (that is, perhaps, the one that tells us the truest things about what the climate will be like at the end of the century, if that is our model's purpose).

To the extent that model constructions depend on human judgement and ability – rather than, for example, being determined by theory – our appraisal of the trustworthiness of a model might depend, at least in part, on the people or groups of people who built the model. Different researchers and groups of researchers have past track records of success, institutional credentials, and so on, and there is no reason that these elements should not affect the degree of trust we can rationally put in their work.

1.3.5 Skill

Mathematical models can help us to reason about the world in myriad ways and can be put to almost infinitely many purposes (as we said, nothing technically stops us from using a model as an art installation). However, models do vary in their degree of adequacy for different purposes. One way of understanding model adequacy for purpose is in terms of model *skill* (Winsberg 2018, chap. 10). Skill refers to a model's adequacy for specific types of epistemic purposes. Three examples of epistemic purposes for which mathematical models may be more or less *skilled* are the following:

(1) *Prediction:* mathematical models can help us to know what a target system will do in the real world at some particular point in time.
(2) *Projection:* mathematical models can help us to estimate what a target system would likely do under different possible counterfactual scenarios, especially under various possible human interventions.
(3) *Causal inference:* mathematical models can help us to learn *what causes what* in a target system. If a model of the climate without increased carbon concentration does not exhibit the warming exhibited by both the real world and models with increased carbon concentration, then we might plausibly infer that the carbon caused the warming (especially if that warming exhibits the same 'fingerprints' in both cases).

As we will see in the next section, sometimes model skill can be measured using specific types of empirical tests. However, at other times no such empirical tests are available, in which case model users must judge a model's skill using other means, often taking into consideration its levels of idealization, articulation, and credentials, among other things. In any case, model skill should be understood on a continuum: that is, when assessing a model for the purpose of prediction, projection, or causal inference, we speak of it being *more or less* skilled.

1.4 Conclusion

In this introductory section, we canvassed a variety of different representational entities in science that are a regularly referred to as 'models'. We noted that this was an extremely heterogeneous collection of entities, but that they could be loosely grouped into four categories: abstract/mental models, concrete models, data models, and mathematical/computational models. We also noted that one thing these entities have in common is that while they are all representational (that is, they all depict the world as being some way or another), few of them are truth apt – the sorts of things we say are 'true'. Rather, they are adequate (or not) for some purpose or another – though often the purpose for which we hope they are adequate includes the purpose of inferring true claims about the world. The models themselves are not truth apt, but often the inferences we draw from them are, and adequacy for purpose often means 'this model is adequate for inferring claims about the world that are likely (enough) to be true to a high (enough) degree of accuracy in a broad (enough) domain of application'. (There'll be much more on this in the next section.)

We next decided to zero in on mathematical and computational models. We saw that models like these are especially useful for the tasks of prediction, projection, and causal inference, and that this, in turn, makes them especially useful and important in guiding decision-making. When this is the case, it's especially helpful to talk about the degree of *skill* that models of this kind have for carrying out these tasks. Skill, we said, is adequacy for a specific kind of quantitative purpose, and evaluating the skill of a model for various purposes is complex and motley – but it often involves looking at the credentials of the model, and the degree to which it is idealized, articulated, and sensitive to the representational choices that we made in creating it.

2 Adequacy for Purpose

2.1 Introduction

In Section 1, we emphasized that our objective is not usually that a model be true, but rather adequate for purpose. This naturally leads to the question: 'what does it *mean* for a model to be adequate for purpose?'. This simple question has a fairly straightforward answer: the model users simply need to trust that they can use the model for whatever tasks they intend to use it for. However, this simple question invites far trickier ones. For example, 'What are all the purposes to which models can be put?'. In fact, models can have myriad purposes: they can be used to make predictions or projections of various kinds, to draw causal inferences, to explain behaviour, to convey things pedagogically, or for something else entirely. Furthermore, when we specify a model's purpose, we usually do so relative to a particular *standard of accuracy*. In other words, we may count a model as adequate for purpose if it gets things right a certain amount of the time, but no less: our model's purpose, then, is cemented to our standard of accuracy. We also tend to specify a model's purpose relative to a particular *domain*. We may trust a model to predict the weather in one geographical region, but not in another, for example. Because of this, a model's purpose may end up being expressed in a rather complicated sort of compound statement: we may intend a model to assist reasoning in x way, to y degree of accuracy, and across z domain of targets. In light of this complexity, articulating all the purposes to which models can be put is a lofty project (and we will not attempt it here). The best we can do is provide illustrative examples, which can help us gain a good understanding of a given model's purpose in context.

An even trickier epistemological question is: 'how do we *decide* when a model is adequate for a specified purpose?'. This question defies a general answer – and we should be very clear that the question of what 'adequacy for purpose' *means* is a different question from how we assess it. In fact, assessing a model's adequacy for purpose requires a good understanding of the model's purpose in context, as well as intimate knowledge of several model attributes, including its levels of idealization, articulation, credentials, and sensitivity, among other things. For example, if using a model requires that it be seeded with initial conditions that reflect the present (or past) state of the world, then our assessment might also depend on the confidence we have in the data models that we treat as initial conditions.

In this section, we explore the topic of model adequacy for purpose by taking a close look at three different models that are used in the Earth and atmospheric sciences: a *zero-dimensional energy balance model*, a *weather forecasting model*, and a *global circulation model of the atmosphere*. As we will see, each of these models is used for a different purpose in a different context, and each has its own special combination of attributes. The first of these models, in particular, is used for what we call an *idealized purpose*, that is, a purpose in the context of Aristotelian idealization. The second and third models, on the other hand, are used for *non-idealized purposes*, which are the same types of epistemic purposes that we associate with model *skill* (Section 1.3.5). The measurement of model skill (or 'adequacy for a non-idealized purpose') raises special epistemological issues in different contexts: in some cases, model skill can be measured operationally; in others, it cannot. In light of these complexities, our discussion of assessing adequacy for purpose proceeds differently for each of the models we explore in this section.

2.2 A Zero-Dimensional Energy Balance Model

One very basic epistemic purpose to which models can be put is *explanation*: models can help us to understand why a target system behaves in the way it does. Consider a very interesting phenomenon we might like to explain: why does Earth have an equilibrium temperature, rather than simply heating up indefinitely and burning up under the Sun? To help explain this, we can use a simple mathematical model called a *zero-dimensional energy balance model* (ZDEBM) (Winsberg 2018). This simple model is described as *zero-dimensional* because it does not allow for any variation in time, nor any variation in space. It simply treats the Earth as the surface of a sphere, as it would look to you if you were looking at it from the surface of the Sun, which is really just a disc. The term *energy balance* in the model's name hints at the useful explanation it provides, which is that Earth reaches an equilibrium temperature thanks to a balance between its incoming and outgoing energy.

As it allows no variation in time and no variation in space, we can already tell that a ZDEBM is a highly *idealized* model. The model strips away properties that are not relevant to the problem at hand, which is to understand why planets achieve equilibrium temperatures. It also involves deliberate distortions, as we will see. However, the model is simple enough that we can reason with it using pencil and paper: it does not require articulation.

The bits of theory and mathematical relationships that fit together in the model come from solar physics, simple optics, and quantum mechanics, which are all well-credentialled sources. Here is how they work together in the model:

- Solar physics tells us how much incoming radiation there is.
- Simple optics tells us that some of that radiation gets reflected into space. We call the rate at which the Earth reflects solar radiation its 'albedo'.
- The Stefan–Boltzmann law of black body radiation tells us how much radiation gets re-radiated back into space. The hotter the disc gets, the more radiation gets sent back.

If we assume that all of these must balance out, we can calculate a target temperature in the following way.

The only sources of incoming and outgoing energy are radiation, which we can measure in watts per square metre (Wm^{-2}). So we have incoming radiative energy, E_{in}, and outgoing radiative energy, E_{out}. And since we want an equilibrium model, we set

$$E_{in} = E_{out}. \tag{1}$$

We call the energy per square metre that the Sun delivers to the Earth the 'Incident solar radiation', S_0.

Since the Earth presents a disc-shaped face to the Sun, it has area πR^2, so it receives $\pi R^2 S_0$ in incoming radiation.

We assume that some fraction of that (which we call the albedo) is reflected back into space and that the remainder $(1-\alpha)$ (the 'co-albedo') is absorbed. We now have a formula for E_{in}:

$$E_{in} = (1 - \alpha)\pi R^2 S_0 \tag{2}$$

To model outgoing energy, the model treats the Earth as a simple, spherical black body that obeys the Stefan–Boltzmann law, which says that a black body will radiate away heat in proportion to the fourth power of the temperature (T, in degrees Kelvin), with the constant of proportionality, σ, called the Stefan–Boltzmann constant. This gives us an equation for E_{out}:

$$E_{out} = 4\pi R^2 \sigma T \tag{3}$$

($4\pi R^2$ being the surface area of a sphere)

Combining equations 1, 2, and 3, and solving for T we get:

$$T = \left(\frac{(1-\alpha)S_0}{4\sigma} \right)^{\frac{1}{4}} \tag{4}$$

Since $S_0 = 1,368 Wm^{-2}$ and $\sigma = 5.67 \times 10^{-8} Wm^{-2}K^{-4}$

we calculate that T = 254.8 K or −18.3°C.

We can call this the Earth's *effective* temperature. Note that this is not equal to the Earth's *actual* temperature, which is more like 15°C: if our goal was to find the Earth's actual temperature, rather than its effective temperature, we would need to alter the model to make it account for the Earth's emissivity.[2] However, the goal of a ZDEBM is not to find Earth's actual temperature. Rather, the purpose of the model is to explain *why planets have an equilibrium temperature* and identify the dominant causal process. The model gives us a very good explanation of this phenomenon: the Earth's ingoing and outgoing energy balance out.

The astute reader might be tempted to interject the following: 'I get that a ZDEBM is being used for explanation rather than prediction, but I still don't understand how a model that gets Earth's equilibrium temperature so wrong could be adequate for any purpose that has to do with the Earth's temperature.' The answer here has to do with Aristotelian idealization. Recall that Aristotelian idealization is when we strip away, in our imagination, factors that we deem unimportant to the system of interest. In such cases, it is helpful, following Martin Jones (2005) and Peter Godfrey-Smith (2009), to think of models that engage in Aristotelian idealization as telling us literally true things about abstract systems. So, on this conception, the ZDEBM is a perfectly accurate model of a perfectly spherical black body immersed for an arbitrarily long time in a uniform field of high frequency radiation. Why should we care about that if we are thinking about the Earth, which is, after all, not a perfectly simple black body, and so on? The reason is that we think that in understanding how such

---

[2] The simplest way we could do this would be to add a simple 'emissivity coefficient' to the model. The emissivity coefficient (call it ε) is defined as the proportion of the energy radiated out by a body relative to what a black body would radiate. There are various ways of measuring the emissivity of the Earth, and they generally settle, for the present time, at around $\epsilon = 0.62$. There are also more complex ways for climate models to account for Earth's emissivity, but they resemble the methods discussed in Section 4 much more than they do the simple model discussed in this section.

a simple, idealized, imaginary system behaves, we get insight both into why the Earth has an equilibrium temperature and regarding one of the most fundamental causal processes involved in determining what it is. In many cases, radical idealization of the kind we see in a ZDEBM is a red flag that a model is unlikely to be adequate for purpose. However, in other cases, we understand the purpose of the model in terms of Aristotelian idealization, and in terms of getting at only *one* of many possible causal processes that are behind a phenomenon we want to understand. In those cases, it is easy to see why radical idealization is not an impediment to adequacy for purpose.

2.3 Weather Forecasting Model

The purpose of weather forecasting models is to make spatially and temporally fine-grained *predictions* about states of the atmosphere over a short time horizon – in other words, to tell us what weather conditions will *actually occur* at a particular time and place in the near future. Compared to the ZDEBM described in Section 2.2, weather forecasting models are far less idealized. In fact, these models are based on a comparatively high degree of fidelity to our understanding of causal relationships in weather systems.

Weather models incorporate both initial conditions and the so-called primitive equations. The primitive equations are a set of non-linear partial differential equations grounded in the well-credentialled theories of fluid mechanics and thermodynamics. Initial conditions are established through a data-driven process: direct measurements of a large number of observable variables that describe the atmosphere and its surroundings in a specified region, such as temperature, precipitation, humidity, atmospheric pressure, wind, and cloud cover. Along with direct measurements of these variables at weather stations, data on initial conditions come from satellite data, aircraft observations, weather balloons, and stream gauges. This measurement process results in a wealth of data, which are often subjected to various smoothing, interpolation, and error correction methods that turn them into standardized datasets (i.e., models of data). These standardized datasets are treated as initial conditions.[3]

The primitive equations are only solvable analytically (i.e., with paper and pencil) in very simple and unrealistic scenarios, which means they have to be turned into equations that can be calculated time-step by time-step on a computer if we actually want to predict the weather. This means weather forecasting models require articulation. Articulation of the equations of this model consists in transforming them into a form that is discrete in both space and time. (In a weather model, the spatial grid size is roughly 10 kilometres and the time-step is a few minutes.)

---

[3] For more detail, see the National Weather Service website, www.weather.gov/about/models.

The discretized version of the equations is supplemented with parameterizations that try to estimate what is happening inside these relatively large grid cells and is therefore lost to the primitive equations. Once the computer model completes these calculations for one time-step, the model can create something that looks just like the initial dataset. This new 'dataset' is fed back into the model, which then runs for another time-step. The model can be used to visualize these data to see what the atmosphere will look like over time. We can also combine (say, by averaging) the forecasts of ensembles of models that rely on different articulations or on different datasets by way of initial conditions. Often the ensemble averages perform better than any single model.

An epistemologically significant thing about weather models is that we can measure their forecasting skill (i.e., their adequacy for *prediction*) fairly objectively with various operationalized metrics. If we use a weather model to make a large number of forecasts and then compare those to what actually happens, we can define measures of forecasting skill like mean absolute error (MAE), bias, and Briar score. These measures tell us, respectively, things like how far the predictions are from what we measured, whether they are systematically wrong in one direction or another, and whether the probabilities they generate match the observed frequencies in the world.[4] This enables us to see how much progress is being made in improving a weather model's forecasting skill over time. The Briar score is especially important because it lends a natural understanding to the probabilities that weather forecasts give us, since they are evaluated with respect to observed frequencies.

In summary, weather models wear their adequacy for purpose on their sleeves: because they are used to predict phenomena that we soon come to observe in great detail, we can measure their skill in a relatively straightforward manner. On the flipside, we can see very easily what weather models are *not* skilled at: as everyone knows, it is impossible to predict whether it will rain on any particular day six months from now. As we will see in Section 2.4, model skill cannot always be measured so straightforwardly as it can in the context of weather models. This raises special epistemological issues, notably in the area of climate science.

2.4 Climate Models

The dynamics of the atmosphere are chaotic. This means that small errors in initial conditions grow very fast when we try to predict the future state of the atmosphere, which explains why predicting the weather more than about 10 days

---

[4] For more detail, see the Meteorological Development Laboratory website, https://vlab.noaa.gov/web/mdl/ndfd-verification-score-definitions.

into the future is nearly impossible for practical purposes. In contrast to 'weather', the very concept of *climate* is tied to a long time horizon: when we speak of a region's climate, we are referring to big-picture trends in the average values of weather variables over periods of at least 30 years. At a high level, then, the purpose of climate models is to produce coarse-grained summaries of weather variables, often in the form of global or continental averages or degrees of variation, and to use this knowledge to help make projections of future climate conditions. To do this, climate models generally do not take into account present weather conditions. (After all, these contribute only to the climate system's internal variability, which is not the target of interest in climate modelling. Worse still, the information contained in a weather dataset is mostly lost after about 10 days of forecasting.) What climate models *do* take into account are the possible effects of various *external forcings*: things like ozone depletion, CO_2 emissions, other greenhouse gases, deforestation, and so on. These are forces that are external to the climate system, but which could push it beyond its normal range of variation – and therefore affect projections of future climate conditions. Of course, there is much uncertainty around these forcings themselves: future CO_2 emissions, for example, depend on numerous unpredictable factors, including (but not limited to) future energy policies and practices. As a result, climate models often consider a range of plausible future scenarios for external forcings, producing projections that correspond to these counterfactual scenarios.

Climate models of the most advanced kind include not only representations of the Earth's atmosphere, but of its hydrosphere (including rivers and seas), cryosphere (ice caps and sheets), land surfaces, and biosphere, as well as the many complex interactions between these systems. Our purposes for such models are almost as complex as the models themselves: we use them to estimate climate sensitivity; to attribute human activities as the cause of observed warming; to project regional changes to the climate under various forcing scenarios; to project sea-level rise; to find possible 'tipping points' in the climate (a critical threshold, the crossing of which leads to dramatic and irreversible changes), and more. While these are some of the many *skills* we hope our climate models will have, we are not quite done spelling out the purposes of climate models. In practice, we have to specify model purposes relative to the degree of accuracy we expect, the degree of confidence we want to have in an answer before we use it, and so on. In climate modelling generally, we face certain obstacles that we must mitigate by *lowering* our standards of adequacy: the chaotic nature of the atmosphere and the long timescales that are of interest to us, for example, mean we must limit what we expect from our models. At best, we hope that climate models will give us averages on time-scales of two to three decades. To mitigate other sources of error, we temper our expectations regarding the degree of accuracy we expect from climate models, asking only for relatively wide uncertainty bands, rather than point forecasts.

An example of an advanced climate model is the Geophysical Fluid Dynamics Laboratory Earth System Model (GFL ESM 4.1). This complex model actually consists of several modules, each corresponding to a different aspect of the climate system. In order to be computationally manageable, all of these modules will necessarily have a much lower degree of fidelity to physical theory than weather prediction models. To show what we mean by this, we can look at just one of the modules in the GFL ESM 4.1, the AM 4.0. The AM 4.0 is an example of a general circulation model of the atmosphere (AGCM), which Winsberg (2018, 44) describes as a 'flagship' climate model. It models the Earth's atmosphere, 'at approximately 1° of resolution with 49 levels of comprehensive, interactive chemistry and aerosols (including aerosol indirect effect) from precursor emissions' (Alvich n.d.a.). By examining how an AGCM specifically is developed, we can get a good idea of how climate models are developed more generally, including the role of *equations*, *discretization*, *parameterization*, and *tuning*.[5]

In principle, the core behaviour of the Earth's atmosphere can be modelled with pencil and paper and three simple equations: (1) Newton's laws of motion as they apply to parcels of fluid; (2) the conservation of mass; and (3) a simple thermodynamic equation that allows us to calculate the heating effect on each parcel of air via a parameterized value of the radiation from the Sun. Unfortunately, this results in a coupled set of non-linear partial differential equations for which we have no closed-form solution. However, if we want a *numerical approximation* of how the atmosphere should behave, we can develop a computer simulation model like an AGCM.

In an AGCM, we transform continuous differential equations into discrete difference equations that approximate them, then we use a computer to solve those equations. At heart, an AGCM is a more coarse-grained version of a weather model. It is more coarse-grained because it has to be run for much longer times. And, of course, because it is more coarse-grained, though its primitive equations might be very close cousins of the weather model's, the degree of articulation it requires is dramatically greater.

Ultimately, an AGCM consists of a three-dimensional grid of cells, with each cell exchanging radiation, heat, moisture, momentum, and mass with its neighbours (Stone and Knutti 2010). In an AGCM, anything that happens below the level of the chosen grid size (i.e., within a grid box) cannot be calculated using the fundamental equations that have been discretized at that grid size. Instead,

---

[5] For more detail, see (Alvich n.d.b.)

any interactions in the system that occur within a grid box need to be treated with a subgrid parameterization. Parameterization refers to the method of using simple mathematical descriptions, that is, equations with parameters, to replace processes that are too small-scale or complex to be physically represented in the discretized model. In climate modelling, parameters are often referred to as 'non-physical', because there are no corresponding values in nature. In developing an AGCM, subgrid parameterizations are chosen and refined based on individual performance; the best value for a parameter in an AGCM is generally an artefact of the computation scheme. Despite being grounded in physical theory, the more a computational model relies on parameterization, the less fidelity to theory the model will exhibit.

The last step in developing an AGCM is *tuning* (Mauritsen et al. 2012). As we use it here, this term refers to the process of adjusting a few key parameter values in order to ensure that the model's *overall* behaviour is acceptable. For example, recall from our discussion of the ZDEBM (Section 2.2) that global warming/cooling will occur whenever there is an imbalance between the amount of solar radiation coming into Earth and the amount of emitted radiation leaving at the top of the atmosphere (TOA). In general, a priority in climate model development is to ensure that the model produces the expected results for TOA energy balance. Model tuning can also be used to ensure that other important model results match expectations (e.g., the general features of atmospheric circulation, observed global mean temperature, tropical variability, and sea-ice seasonality). Understanding how a climate model is tuned is key to understanding how we assess its adequacy for purpose.

With that preamble in mind, what do we look to when we evaluate whether climate models are adequate for our purposes? As with a weather model, we can evaluate a climate model on various metrics of observable skill, such as bias (see Section 2.3). But unlike a weather model, measured skill cannot be the be-all and end-all of climate model appraisal, for a number of reasons. First of all, we hope to use our climate models to forecast how the climate will evolve under conditions we have never seen before. The fact that a climate model exhibits skill under the conditions we are now experiencing is no guarantee that it will do so under future forcings. Even for present conditions, assessing the skill of a climate model is more difficult than assessing the skill of a weather model because we don't have nearly as much relevant data. We can evaluate the skill of a weather model nearly every day, but we can only evaluate a climate model roughly a decade at a time, and we only have a handful of decades of good data to compare against – with even fewer than that having occurred after the first climate models came into service.

Furthermore, insofar as we want to get probabilities out of a climate model, we can't possibly measure anything like a Briar score because we don't have multiple trials of the same set-ups. A weather forecaster makes predictions under similar situations multiple times, so if it predicts a 70% chance of rain under those conditions, we can check to see whether rain occurs 70% of the time. But nothing comparable happens in climate, so the probabilities we infer from climate models are more difficult to interpret and understand.

Perhaps most importantly, we want to use climate models to tell us what will happen under various different counterfactual scenarios; for example, those defined by possible emissions pathways. This is the only way we can use a climate model to help us decide if the expense of pursuing a particular scenario – for example, an emissions pathway associated with a more demanding policy change mandating less fossil fuel use – is worth the cost. And to be effective at doing this, we have to be able to trust a climate model to tell us not only how the world will actually behave, but also how it *would have behaved* under emissions pathways that never came to be.

As a result, much more than in the case of weather models, we have to look at the *internal qualities* of a climate model very carefully in order to appraise whether it is adequate for our purposes. What qualities do we look at? There's a long list, beginning with the model's fidelity to well-established theory and the mathematical arguments for the trustworthiness of steps we take in articulating our basic model into its computational form. We also perform sensitivity analyses: we can check to see what degree of sensitivity our models display to choices of parameters about which we have substantial uncertainty. If a climate model needs a mathematical function to estimate a particular subgrid parameter (e.g., cloud formation), and we are uncertain what the best form of that function is, we can explore how sensitive the model is to different values that we might pick. If the model is highly sensitive to the value we choose, and we think that several different values are equally reasonable, we can temper our expectations concerning the accuracy of our projections by widening our confidence intervals.

Another strategy we use is ensemble studies: different models not only have different parameter values, but they have different model structures. We can try to do for model structure the same things we do for parameter values, though the situation here gets a bit more complex. The basic idea is that climate research centres around the world produce a variety of different models. Some of these models differ from each other in ways that are deeper than simply having different values for parameters plugged in. We describe such models as having different 'model structures'. The idea is that by looking at which results come out the same in all members of the ensemble we might be able to learn something about whether we can trust those results. This is all far from straightforward, however, and a large literature exists on how to manage this source of knowledge (Abramowitz et al. 2019). There are other more bespoke techniques that climate scientists turn to, including trying to achieve process understanding and employing emergent constraints (see Knutti (2018) and Winsberg (2018, chap. 12) for more details).

And of course, we are free to declare that the models are *not* adequate for some of the purposes we hoped they would be. Indeed, there is some controversy about how adequate climate models are for forecasting the melting of land ice, projecting regional conditions like precipitation levels, and foreseeing the likely impacts on major climatic structures, such as the thermohaline circulation and the El Niño–Southern Oscillation cycle. Alternatively, we can declare that our models are adequate for certain purposes only in conjunction with other lines of evidence. For example, many climate scientists would say that climate models are adequate for the purpose of informing, *along with other sources of evidence*, an estimate of equilibrium climate sensitivity (ECS), the amount we expect the world to warm under a doubling of CO_2 in an uncertainty band that is about 3°C wide. But some would hesitate to claim that, *on their own*, climate models would be adequate for that purpose.

2.5 Conclusion

In this section, we have looked closely at three different kinds of models and used them to illustrate three very different ways in which we can assess a model's adequacy for purpose. While this is not meant to be a complete and exhaustive taxonomy of such assessment methods, it does illustrate how varied these methods are. In the first case, adequacy for purpose is argued for by limiting the model's intended purpose to giving extremely idealized explanations of phenomena. In the second, it is argued for by repeatedly testing the predictions of the model, scoring it on a variety of metrics of skill, and then carefully circumscribing our attributions of skill for the model to the kinds of predictions or forecasts on which the model scores well. In the last case, the situation is entirely motley and nearly impossible to fully analyse. When dealing with a complex real-world projection model like a climate model – a highly idealized and articulated model that is intended to make counterfactual claims about the future – determining adequacy for purpose requires an examination of a wide array of features of the model. It also requires being quite careful and circumscribed about what purposes we take the model to be adequate *for*.

3 Inadequacy for Purpose

3.1 Introduction

On 1 May 2020, evolutionary biologist and modelling expert Carl Bergstom and biostatistician Natalie Dean published an op-ed piece in the *New York Times*

(Bergstrom and Dean 2020). Written at the start of the Covid-19 pandemic, its title contained a warning: 'What the Proponents of "Natural" Herd Immunity Don't Say: Try to Reach It without a Vaccine, and Millions will Die.' In the article, Bergstrom and Dean calculated a value called the 'herd immunity threshold', which, as they explained, is a concept typically described in the context of a vaccine. 'When enough people are vaccinated', they wrote,

> a pathogen cannot spread easily through the population. If you are infected with measles but everyone you interact with has been vaccinated, transmission will be stopped in its tracks. Vaccination levels must stay above a threshold that depends upon the transmissibility of the pathogen. We don't yet know exactly how transmissible the coronavirus is, but say each person infects an average of three others. That would mean nearly two-thirds of the population would need to be immune to confer herd immunity. (Bergstrom and Dean 2020)

In the absence of a vaccine (as was the case in May 2020), Bergstrom and Dean stressed, immunity to the virus would only be achieved through infection and this would lead to a lot of deaths. More deaths, even, than we might think. After all, new infections would continue for some time even after the herd immunity threshold was reached, an epidemiological phenomenon called *overshoot*.

In this section, we examine Bergstrom and Dean's op-ed, alongside related arguments on social media, in order to build on our discussion of model adequacy for purpose and introduce the topic of values in modelling. As we will show, although Bergstrom and Dean's op-ed explains epidemiological phenomena that a simple model can help us understand, it also draws conclusions that go far beyond what that model can tell us. This case study raises a broader question: what is the significance of building and using models for purposes for which they are not adequate?

3.2 SIR Models: From Overshoot to Lockdown?

In their op-ed, Bergstrom and Dean (2020) focus first on estimating the herd immunity threshold in the context of Covid-19 and explaining the concept of overshoot. The origin of these concepts is a simple mathematical model called an 'SIR' model ('Susceptible, Infected, Removed') (Britton 2010; Handel, Longini, and Antia 2007). This highly idealized model represents the dynamics between people in the context of an infectious disease, with each of three groups represented in its own 'compartment':

- **Susceptible**: The number of people who have not yet been infected with a pathogen and are therefore vulnerable to infection.
- **Infectious**: The number of people who are infected and capable of infecting others.

- **Removed:** The number of people who are no longer capable of infecting others or being infected (e.g., because they have recovered from the disease or died). This compartment may also be called 'recovered' or 'resistant'.

In a SIR model, when a susceptible individual and an infectious individual come into 'infectious contact', the susceptible person becomes infected and moves from the S compartment to the I compartment (or, in some models, does so with some probability). Over time, infectious individuals also move from the 'Infectious' to the 'Removed' compartment. There are a number of different ways of giving this kind of model its dynamics – that is, of providing the mathematics of how the system will evolve over time such that people will gradually move from the S to the I to the R compartment. The most standard form of the dynamics looks like this:

The transition rate between S and I is given by:

$$dS/dt = -\beta SI \tag{1}$$

where

β is the average rate of potentially infecting contacts a single person has per unit time multiplied by the probability that actual infection would occur between an infected person and a susceptible person.

And the transition rate between I and R is given by:

$$dR/dt = -\gamma I \tag{2}$$

where

γ is the fraction of infected people who recover per unit time.

In a SIR model, we begin by assuming that mixing in human populations is homogeneous: that is, every individual potentially encounters every other individual and, *ceteris paribus*, every infected individual will infect a given number of random new people. This number is parameterized with the parameter R_0. In other words, at the very beginning of the epidemic (time 0) we expect every infected individual to infect R_0 many new individuals (e.g., $R_0 = 5$). (That is, when Bergstrom and Dean say, 'We don't yet know exactly how transmissible the coronavirus is, but say each person infects an average of three others', they are imagining an R_0 of 3.)

As time goes on, a SIR model shows, the number of infected individuals will increase and the number of susceptible individuals will decrease – meaning each infected individual has fewer potential people to infect. We can call the proportion of the population that is susceptible, at time t, 'S_t' and the 'effective reproduction number', at time t, 'R_t', which is equal to $R_0 * S_t$. In simple terms, if, at the beginning of an epidemic, we expected each infected person to infect 5 people (i.e., $R_0 = 5$), but now only 80% or 0.8 of the population is susceptible, then we will expect each infected person to infect only $5 * 0.8 = 4$ new people.

Once R_t falls below one, each new infected person will infect less than one new person in turn –at that point, the epidemic will wane. In fact, R_t will fall below one when S reaches a threshold of $S_{threshold} = 1/R_0$, which is when $1-S = 1-1/R_0$. And $1-S$ is simply the number of people who have already either been infected or vaccinated. So, in this simple model, $1/(1-R_0)$ is what is considered the 'herd immunity threshold'.

A simple SIR model can also show that the rate of new infections doesn't immediately grind to a halt once the herd immunity threshold is reached. Rather, the first derivative of the rate of new infections turns negative for the first time, representing a rate of decay rather than a rate of growth. In fact, the number of susceptibles can fall well below the threshold $S_{threshold}$. This additional depletion of susceptibles is what is referred to as 'overshoot' (Handel, Longini, and Antia 2007).

In much the same way that we can use a highly idealized ZDEBM to calculate the effective temperature of the Earth (see Section 2), we can use a simple SIR model to explain why certain infectious disease epidemics will eventually wane and why new infections do not stop abruptly when the herd immunity threshold is reached. However, it is important to emphasize that a SIR model is a 'very strong oversimplification' of any real infectious disease outbreak (Handel, Longini, and Antia 2007). In fact, real outbreaks involve stochasticity, take place among populations with heterogeneous clinical characteristics and social contact networks, and have many other complicating features, such as the potential for pathogens to exhibit seasonality (Chikina and Pegden 2020; Choi, Tuel, and Eltahir 2021; Handel, Longini, and Antia 2007; Rucinski et al. 2020).

The fact that none of this complexity is represented in simple SIR models limits the range of purposes to which these models can be put. To mitigate this, modellers will often build additional features onto simple SIR models. For example, modellers will often add an 'exposed' or 'E' group, representing the group of people who have been exposed to an infectious pathogen, but who are in a latency period and not quite ready to infect new people. In such a model, sometimes called a 'SEIR' model, people will transition from susceptible to exposed before finally becoming infected. A SEIR model with a substantial latency period will already exhibit less overshoot than a simple SIR model. In the most complex adaptations to SIR models, modellers aim to represent the fact that real populations display a complex network structure and heterogeneous mixing, which greatly influences infectious disease dynamics, including the herd immunity threshold (Britton, Ball, and Trapman 2020).

In their op-ed, Bergstrom and Dean (2020) do not mention SIR models directly, but these models are the source of the simple method they use to estimate the herd immunity threshold and establish the risk of overshoot. Importantly, a simple SIR model allows us to calculate the herd immunity threshold in much the same way a ZDEBM allows us to calculate the effective (but not *actual*) temperature of the Earth. Just as a ZDEBM does not account for the Earth's emissivity, a simple SIR model does not account for things like stochasticity, seasonality, and heterogeneous population mixing: hence, the results of each model come with a strong *ceteris paribus* clause. Neither is adequate for making real-world projections of quantitative outcomes under counterfactual scenarios, or for establishing conclusions like Bergstrom and Dean's in their op-ed.

In particular, Bergstrom and Dean (2020) assume that once an infectious disease outbreak has begun, in the absence of external control measures, it will continue unabated until the herd immunity threshold is reached, and even beyond. This assumption is represented in the figure that accompanies the op-ed, which depicts a logistic increase in infections. The figure even includes a timescale in days and a representation of the percentage of total infections that would be due to overshoot, though SIR models are not adequate for the purpose of predicting these quantitative outcomes. Again, the many factors that complicate epidemics but are not represented in SIR models make it impossible for us to use simple SIR models for these purposes. Nothing like what the figure predicts happened anywhere in the world, because a simple SIR model was nowhere near adequate for predicting the spread of SARS-CoV-2. Bergstrom and Dean's (2020) claim that 'If the pandemic went uncontrolled in the United States, it *could* [our emphasis] continue for months after herd immunity was reached, infecting many more millions in the process' is similar to the claim that the Earth *could* have stopped warming at -15°C. Insofar as these are claims that could be taken to be true, they are simply claims about how a world would behave under highly unrealistic *ceteris paribus* conditions. Otherwise, a claim like 'it could continue for months' is an empty modal with seemingly only rhetorical significance.

Following their discussion of herd immunity and overshoot, Bergstrom and Dean (2020) went on to make remarks about pandemic mitigation. They noted that some countries had attempted strategies intended to safely build up population immunity to Covid-19 without a vaccine. For example, they noted, Sweden had advised older people and other special groups to self-quarantine, but kept many schools, restaurants, and bars open – and many commentators had suggested that similar policies would be good for poorer countries like India. But given the fatality rate of Covid-19, Bergstrom and Dean (2020) stressed, '*there would be no way to do this without huge numbers of casualties*' (italics added). On these grounds, they argued that it was too early to proceed as if most people would inevitably become infected, and that we should not trust our ability to achieve a 'controlled burn' of the pandemic. Instead, Bergstrom and Dean (2020) emphasized that aggressive control and containment could be used to reduce strain on the healthcare system and to buy the scientific community time to develop treatments, vaccines, and so on. (It is, of course, noteworthy that although Sweden continued the policy discussed by Bergstrom and Dean, its number of casualties was not an outlier relative to European countries that pursued the aggressive mitigation strategies they had in mind.) These arguments echoed one that Bergstrom had made on social media the month before, in which he drew on a SEIR model to support the idea of instituting a 30-day 'lockdown' at the peak of an epidemic:

> If one can break the momentum that is driving the epidemic beyond the herd immunity threshold, one can reduce that overshoot substantially. Below, I've modelled a 30 day period of social distancing around the epidemic peak, that drops R0 from 2.5 to 0.3. This 30 day lockdown period is far less onerous than that required to hold the virus in check until a vaccine is available but reduces the total fraction infected from 90% to 70% by eliminating much of the overshoot. In my view, this is not a substitute for aggressive control and containment, because 60% of the population still becomes infected. In India, for example, this would cost about 19 million lives with a 2% infection fatality rate. But the 30 day lockdown would save >5 million. (Bergstrom on Twitter, 19 April 2020; cited in Winsberg 2022)

This argument turns on several precise quantitative claims, including a specific reduction in infections that could be achieved with a 30-day lockdown. Yet such precise quantitative claims go beyond what a simple SEIR model can tell us, as we have shown, and are highly sensitive to inputs like the infection fatality rate, here assumed to be 2%, though assumed to be 0.5%–1% in Bergstrom and Dean's (2020) op-ep. (The true global average of this value is controversial, but is probably much closer to the lower end of Bergstrom and Dean's estimate, if not slightly below it, and substantially lower than the 2% estimate Bergstrom used in his social media thread.[6]) They are also highly sensitive to whether or not the model contains the kinds of mechanisms that seem to make respiratory viral pathogens come in waves, even in the absence of human interventions. In the remainder of this section, we discuss the social and ethical significance of building and using scientific models for purposes for which they are not adequate, placing this in the context of philosophy's values in science literature.

---

[6] See Covid-19 Forecasting Team (2022).

We also discuss what sorts of considerations are important when using scientific models to inform public policy decisions, such as implementing the public health measures that Bergstrom and Dean (2020) endorsed.

3.3 Two Kinds of Risk

As we established in Section 1, models are not perfectly complete and entirely accurate representations of target systems. By necessity, modelling involves representational decisions – overlapping decisions about *what to represent* and *how to represent it* – which are driven by the purpose of the model (Harvard and Winsberg 2022). For example, as we have seen, it is not always necessary to represent every complicating factor in a model of an infectious disease epidemic. If a model's purpose is to explain why some infectious disease epidemics exhibit a herd immunity threshold, the simplest SIR model will be adequate for this purpose. However, if a model's purpose is to make a quantitative prediction regarding the number of infections that will be observed over a specific time period under various human interventions, the simplest SIR model will not do. If our goal was to build a model adequate for this purpose, we would have to represent many, if not all, of the complicating factors discussed in Section 2.2 (and possibly more). Indeed, it is possible that even the very best infectious disease model we could build would only be adequate for the purpose of making quantitative predictions if we defined that purpose conservatively, such that we accepted predictions with very large margins of error. In any case, our decision concerning *what* factors to represent in the model would be informed, at least in part, by how *accurate* we wanted our quantitative predictions to be, which we can think of as part of our model's purpose (see Section 2). And whatever complicating factors we decide to represent – say, for example, heterogeneity in social contact rates – will present us with further decisions regarding *how* to represent them. For example, deciding to include heterogeneity in social contact rates means we will have to decide which source of data or evidence is adequate to represent this phenomenon.

The purpose of this subsection is to reflect on the ways in which representational decisions in modelling are *value-laden*.[7] There are at least three ways for us to disentangle and appreciate this. First, representational decisions correspond to the purpose of the model and *purposes* are value-laden. Second, even with a set purpose, judgements about what is *adequate* for that purpose are

---

[7] When we say representational decisions are value-laden, we mean they are the sorts of 'scientific choices that cannot be decided solely by appealing to evidence and logic' (Elliott 2017, 11). In other words, we mean that representational decisions invoke *social values*, that is, 'the estimations of any agent or group of agents of what is important and valuable – in the typical social and ethical senses – and of what is to be avoided, and to what degree' (Winsberg 2012, 112).

value-laden, especially when model skill cannot be measured operationally. Third, representational decisions influence model results, which affect our 'inferential decisions' concerning which facts to endorse at the stage of model interpretation, the moment at which we use the model to infer facts about the world (Harvard et al. 2021). This means representational decisions influence our risk of endorsing a false fact, which is what we call *inductive risk* (Harvard and Winsberg 2022).[8]

Inductive risk highlights the role of social and ethical values in model interpretation, since we put these in play when deciding what facts to endorse as true, taking into account the possible harms of endorsing a false fact; if we evaluate those harms as serious, our ethical values tell us to demand a higher standard of evidence. However, our values come into play in modelling well before model interpretation, and value-laden representational decisions are distinct from decisions around which facts to endorse – after all, representational decisions are generally about what is adequate for purpose, not about what is true. In modelling, then, it is useful to think in terms of two types of risk: while inductive risk is the risk of endorsing a false fact, *representational risk* is the risk of making a representational decision that is inadequate for purpose. These two types of risk are not unrelated because an inadequate representational decision will sometimes lead to a downstream endorsement of a false fact. Yet, (1) *it needn't* lead to this and (2) it can also lead to *other harms* that are distinct from a false conclusion. These distinct harms include lamentably incomplete scientific results, irrelevant or distracting results, and even pernicious and unjust gaps in scientific knowledge (Harvard and Winsberg 2022). The two types of risk therefore encourage us to distinguish between the influence of values in model development/selection (i.e., in managing representational risk) and in model interpretation (i.e., in managing inductive risk), respectively.

To help appreciate the role of values in modelling, we can think about the risks that Bergstrom and Dean (2020) and Bergstrom (on Twitter, 19 April 2020) were running in their op-ed and social media threads, respectively. In both cases, Bergstrom and Dean were making representational decisions (i.e., to use simple SIR and SEIR models, respectively, which are adequate for some purposes, but not for others, as well as to choose certain parameters for the models) and inferential decisions (i.e., decisions about what facts to endorse as true). This means we can use both the representational risk and inductive risk 'lenses' to analyse what social and ethical considerations would have been relevant to Bergstrom and Dean's decisions.

---

[8] The term 'inductive risk' was first used by Carl Hempel (1954) and more recently revived by Heather Douglas (2000, 2009). There is considerable debate around how to define inductive risk (Elliott and Richards 2017), but here we follow Harvard and Winsberg (2022).

Let's start with inductive risk, by identifying some 'facts' that Bergstrom and Dean (2020) and Bergstrom (on Twitter, 19 April 2020) endorsed. We might want to consider the claim that a 30-day lockdown period 'reduces the total fraction infected from 90% to 70% by eliminating much of the overshoot' and that in India this 'would save >5 million' lives assuming a 2% fatality rate (Bergstrom on Twitter, 19 April 2020). To analyse the inductive risk here, we must consider the possible harms of endorsing this 'fact' (which turned out to be far from true). Thus, we should keep in mind that the claim is both highly precise and explicitly made in the context of endorsing a public health intervention that is known to present potential harms as well as potential benefits, as most health interventions do. In health policy-making and decision-making, the conventional approach is to quantify both potential harms and benefits and evaluate whether the intervention would be net beneficial. How accurately potential harms and benefits are quantified is therefore of great importance. If, for example, a 30-day lockdown (which affects all or most of the population) were to reduce the total fraction infected from 40% to 30%, or from 30% to 20%, rather than from 90% to 70%, this may flip the results of a harm–benefit analysis (i.e., change the policy recommendation). Deciding to endorse the fact that a 30-day lockdown period '*reduces* the total fraction infected from 90% to 70%' (italics added) therefore *specifically* involves ethical considerations. In particular, it involves considering whether a simple SEIR model is adequate to provide evidence strong enough to endorse this fact, or whether the seriousness of a factual error in this context means other evidence is required.

Instead of focusing on Bergstrom's decision to endorse a fact, we can focus on his decision to use a simple SEIR model to: (1) predict the impact of a 30-day lockdown on total Covid-19 infections over 140 days, and (2) inform the decision to implement a 30-day lockdown in India. As we interpret it, these are two purposes to which Bergstrom put his SEIR model. In this context, the relevant risk is *representational risk*, the risk that a simple SEIR model will be inadequate for these purposes. With respect to purpose (1), representational risk is high because the model's precise quantitative predictions depend on highly *unconstrained* 'what to represent' and 'how to represent' decisions. Specifically, the model excludes information about many factors that complicate epidemics and incorporates both a highly controversial estimate of the Covid-19 infection fatality rate (i.e., 2%) and a highly *idealized* assumption about epidemic growth (i.e., in the absence of interventions, Covid-19 infections would follow logistic growth all the way to the herd immunity threshold and then continue into overshoot over a very short period of time – with 60% of people infected on the order of 60 days). Perhaps the most salient harm that could result if the SEIR model were inadequate for purpose (1) is that its inaccurate results would mislead people. In this context, representational risk and inductive risk seem to be entangled: both link to the harm of endorsing a false fact. However, with respect to purpose (2), representational risk links to a distinct harm, as we will see.

We interpreted purpose (2) of Bergstrom's SEIR model in terms of decision-making: the purpose of informing the decision to implement a 30-day lockdown in India. In the decision-making context, it is not only important that a model's quantitative predictions are accurate, but that it represents all of the information that is relevant to the decision. Importantly, what information is relevant to a decision is a highly value-laden question: we can imagine, for example, that some decision-makers would desire only information about the effect of a 30-day lockdown on total number of Covid-19 infections, but that other decision-makers would desire information about the effect of the lockdown on food insecurity, educational outcomes, all-cause mortality, and so on. In light of this, we can see that whether or not Bergstrom's SEIR model is adequate for purpose (2) depends directly on the *model users* and their moral values around how decisions about public health interventions should be made. If model users desire only information about the effect of a 30-day lockdown on total number of Covid-19 infections, Bergstrom's SEIR model would be adequate for the purpose of decision-making if its quantitative predictions were accurate. However, if model users desire information about the effect of a lockdown on food insecurity, educational outcomes, and all-cause mortality in order to inform their decision, then Bergstrom's SEIR model would not be adequate for purpose, regardless of how accurate it were at predicting Covid-19 deaths. In this context, the harm at stake is best understood as *incomplete* results rather than factually incorrect results. After all, even if the model's quantitative predictions were precisely accurate, the model could still be inadequate for purpose if model users' decision-making approach demanded information on all the potential harms of lockdown. Depending on our moral values, and perhaps our knowledge about the ultimate effects of lockdown in India (Shanker and Raghavan 2021), we may consider such incompleteness in model results to be more or less harmful, somewhere between lamentable and unjust.

3.4 Models for Public Decisions

In the last subsection, we emphasized that our social and ethical values are in play (1) when deciding what to represent in a model and how to represent it; and (2) when deciding what facts to endorse on the basis of model results. We also emphasized that model purposes can be spelled out at different levels:

sometimes, a model can be understood as being for the purpose of quantitative prediction at one level, but for the purpose of *public decision-making* at a higher level. Models that may be used to inform public decisions raise special moral considerations, not least because their adequacy for purpose depends directly on model users and *their* moral values concerning how public decisions should be made; yet modellers and model users are not always directly connected. Sometimes, modellers work directly with model users and build models that are explicitly informed by the latter's values around decision-making. At other times, modellers have no direct connection to model users, but rather build models according to their own values around decision-making. Under these conditions, models have the potential to be used as rhetorical devices, which raises further moral considerations. In this subsection, we outline just a few different possible approaches to public decision-making and establish that models must be built very differently in order to be adequate to support each one.

Consider, for example, three possible approaches to deciding whether to implement a 30-day lockdown in India. Following the first, the decision depends uniquely on whether a 30-lockdown is likely to prevent Covid-19 infections; we ignore all other considerations. Following the second, we still ignore all other considerations, but now we require that a 30-day lockdown is likely to prevent a *certain minimum number* of Covid-19 infections. And following the third, the decision depends on whether a 30-lockdown is likely to be net beneficial, taking into account a broad range of harms and benefits. The first of these approaches assumes a duty to prevent Covid-19 infections, period, and the second assumes a duty to prevent a certain number of Covid-19 infections, if possible (cf. Harvard and Winsberg 2021).The third does not assume any straightforward, singular duties of these kinds, but rather assumes that decisions should be net beneficial from some perspective. To inform the first decision-making approach, it would not be necessary to build a model capable of quantitative prediction (indeed, it may not be necessary or appropriate to build a model at all). However, to inform the other two decision-making approaches, a model would have to be adequate for quantitative prediction. Both of these decision-making approaches, then, raise a further value-laden question, which pertains to the existence of *uncertainty* surrounding quantitative predictions. Such uncertainty is particularly inevitable when modelling complex, non-linear systems like epidemics. Because there is generally a good deal of uncertainty around the harms and benefits of health interventions, conventional approaches to health modelling for decision-making typically combine something like a cost–benefit analysis with uncertainty analysis (Briggs, Sculpher, and Claxton 2006).

As we saw, the SIR and SEIR models that Bergstrom and Dean (2020) and Bergstrom (on Twitter, 19 April 2020) presented in their op-ed and social media threads, respectively, do not represent potential harms associated with social distancing policies/lockdowns or estimate the uncertainty around their predictions. As a result, their models are adequate only for certain model users: those who consider only the number of Covid-19 infections averted to be relevant to the decision and who are unconcerned by uncertainty. It is also apparent that Bergstrom and Dean's models were built by them independently, rather than in collaboration with model users, such as those responsible for deciding whether or not to implement a 30-day lockdown in India. As a result, there is some risk that Bergstrom and Dean's models could be perceived as having a rhetorical purpose – for example, the purpose of persuading people to implement a 30-day lockdown in India. To see why there would be a risk of such a rhetorical purpose being perceived, it is useful to think about what the dialectical situation was (at least for some people) regarding lockdowns generally. In early 2020, some people were arguing that lockdowns would cause more harm than good, because of their negative impact on the economy, education, and so on. However, this view was not very popular among public health professionals (and perhaps the typical *New York Times* reader), at least not with respect to the developed world. The thought was that lockdowns would surely achieve more good via saved lives than they would cause harm via decreased general welfare. Many people were willing to conclude this simply on the basis of their moral intuitions.

However, it was sometimes acknowledged that the calculus could be considerably different in developing economies like India and South Africa, due to the fact that overall welfare is much closer to dangerously low levels for a large majority of people (Broadbent 2020; Broadbent and Streicher 2022). Bergstrom himself effectively acknowledged this: 'Every possible measure should be taken to prevent this [unprecedented humanitarian disaster] from happening. Yet in some countries this may be unavoidable. Some nations may simply lack the economic resources, technological capacity, and political will to contain the virus until a vaccine can be developed.' (Bergstrom on Twitter, 19 April 2020; cited in Winsberg 2022). Indeed, it was reasonable to worry that even if developing countries could sustain lockdowns as long as developed countries (a dubious proposition), vaccines would be rolled out very slowly in developing countries anyway. Thus, Bergstrom was aware that the central question regarding lockdowns in developing countries was not 'Should they lockdown until a vaccine is developed?', but rather 'Should they try a relatively short lockdown?'. One prima facie reasonable response to this would be to point out that a lockdown that lasts only a tenth or less of the time needed to make a vaccine available would be pointlessly harmful, so it was clear that a special argument would be needed for the case of the developing world. This is what Bergstrom's SEIR model appears to provide in representing the phenomenon of 'overshoot', along with a very high infection fatality rate of 2% (a rate 2 to 4 times higher than the one he and Dean used in the *New York Times* piece (Bergstrom and Dean 2020)). In other words, it could be perceived that Bergstrom's SEIR model was serving the rhetorical purpose of presenting a quantitative prediction so nuclear that it would obviate the need for more a complex cost–benefit model.

3.5 Conclusion

In this section, we have looked closely at an application of a SIR/SEIR model, both to illustrate ways in which models can be used for purposes for which they are not adequate and to tie this to the fact that building and using models invokes social and ethical values. We showed that there are two risks associated with building and using a model for a specific purpose: the risk associated with drawing false inferences from the model (inductive risk), and the risk associated with making representational decisions that are inadequate for purpose (representational risk). Both of these risks are moral. In the first case, the risk is moral because when we use a model to infer a conclusion, and endorse that conclusion as being a fact, harms and benefits can ensue. This means that deciding whether to endorse a fact requires reflection on the harms of endorsing the fact when it is false and on the harms of not endorsing the fact when it is true. In the second case, the risk is moral because making representational decisions that are inadequate for purpose can not only increase inductive risk, but also lead to harms that are distinct from a false conclusion.

We also suggested, at the end of this section, that Bergstrom and Dean's (2020) model could be perceived as having served a rhetorical purpose. In particular, we noted that the model might be perceived as being used to make a special argument for lockdowns in the case of the developing world. Thus, we seem to have encountered a new purpose for models, one that goes beyond the purposes we canvassed in Section 2: models can be used rhetorically to advance arguments for conclusions that the model-makers want to advance. This points to a current controversy in the values in modelling literature: when is it legitimate to use a model for a rhetorical purpose?

One way we can think about a rhetorical purpose for models is in terms of a model's purpose being its 'performativity' or 'performative' impact (Basshuysen et al. 2021). The performative impact of a model is the degree to which it encourages people to change their behaviour and/or compels policy-makers to adopt various policies. That models may have the purpose of performativity has been discussed in the epidemiology literature: Biggs and Littlejohn (2021), for example, remark that '[i]nitial projections [of a Covid-19 model] built in worst-case scenarios that would never happen as a means of spurring leadership into action' (92), and Ioannidis, Cripps, and Tanner (2022) speculate that '[i]n fact, erroneous predictions may have even been useful. A wrong, doomsday prediction may incentivize people towards better personal hygiene.' Some philosophers have suggested that, even if a model makes very poor predictions or projections, we might want, under some conditions, to consider a model's performative impact to be a potential virtue (Basshuysen et al. 2021). Designating a model's performative impact as a virtue under some conditions equates to sanctioning a model's use for rhetorical purposes under those conditions (Winsberg and Harvard 2022).

While some authors have suggested that using models for rhetorical purposes is sometimes acceptable, others have argued that this practice should be strictly avoided. Although there may be a temptation to encourage people and/ or policy-makers to adopt certain behaviour, Winsberg and Harvard (2022) argue that modellers should not try to do so by incorporating worst-case scenarios or other specific types of predictions into models. One reason for this is that changes in behaviour often have *costs*, including both financial costs and other undesirable, unintended effects, which can be difficult to anticipate and even harder to quantify. Indeed, one of the most important functions of policy-oriented modelling is to facilitate a cost–benefit analysis, which encourages careful reflection on the potential downstream effects of behaviour change, the methods available to quantify those effects, and the inevitable uncertainty that will surround the results. In other words, one of the core functions of models is to help us determine *with greater accuracy and reliability* which behaviours are truly the best ones for us to adopt, given the values we attach to different potential outcomes. It should be clear, then, that using models to promote a certain course of action from the outset runs counter to that core function, and puts us at risk of adopting behaviours that do not actually accord with our values. Furthermore, Winsberg and Harvard (2022) argue, to use models for a rhetorical purpose runs the risk of undermining the credibility of science, as well the right of the public to have policies that reflect their own values (not just those of model developers). The question of whether it is acceptable for models to be used for rhetorical purposes remains a topic of debate in the values in modelling literature. In the next section, we will canvass considerations in favour of the claim that the public deserves a say in how models should be developed and used to inform public policy.

4 Models and Values

4.1 Introduction

In Section 3, we introduced the topic of values in modelling by establishing that scientific models give rise to two kinds of risk. First, during model development, there is representational risk: the risk that modellers will make representational decisions (i.e., decisions about *what to represent* and *how to represent it*) that will be inadequate for the intended purpose of the model. Second, during model interpretation, there is inductive risk: the risk that model users will make inferential decisions (i.e., decisions about *what to endorse as a fact*) that will be erroneous. Because social and ethical values come into play in deciding how to manage these risks, we said that the processes of model development and interpretation are value-laden. In this section, we revisit this topic in more detail, showing how we can follow Harvard and Winsberg (2022) and Harvard et al. (2021) in developing a basic framework to identify and understand value judgements in modelling generally. We then apply this framework to the Imperial College London (ICL) 'CovidSim' model, a well-known model used to estimate the impact of non-pharmaceutical interventions (NPIs) on Covid-19 mortality and healthcare demand (Ferguson et al. 2020). Building on this detailed account of value judgements in a single model, we end our discussion by considering how model-building can proceed in an ethical manner, particularly when the goal of modelling is to inform public policy.

4.2 A Basic 'Values in Modelling' Framework

As we discussed in Section 3, representational decisions in modelling take the form of overlapping decisions about *what to represent* and *how to represent it*. Roughly speaking, we can think of 'what to represent' decisions as concerning *what entities to include in and exclude from a model* and 'how to represent' decisions as about *what methods to use to represent entities chosen for inclusion in a model*. But, as Harvard et al. (2021) acknowledge, these decisions are closely intertwined in practice. For example, 'what to represent' decisions are routinely informed by *how* or *whether* the representation of something can be achieved: if modellers would like to include an entity in a model, but have no data to support doing so, they may decide to exclude it. In this case, the *how to represent* decision affects the *what to represent* decision. Indeed, the distinction between 'what to represent' and 'how to represent' is mostly a practical distinction, rather than a philosophical or theoretical one. Much of what we say in what follows applies equally to both types of representational decisions, and often it makes sense to simply speak of 'representational decisions' in general. However, the practical distinction between 'what to represent' and 'how to represent' decisions can be useful for structuring an initial discussion about modelling decisions, which helps us to see the value-laden (and iterative) character of these decisions.

4.2.1 What to Represent: A High-Level View

In their initial discussion of 'what to represent' decisions, Harvard et al. (2021) invite us to think in the big picture: they note that 'social and ethical values shape our views about what is necessary or important – or even acceptable – to reason about using scientific models'. In other words, the foremost 'what to represent' decision in modelling concerns what topic to study, which is long-recognized to reflect social and ethical values (Longino 1990; Weber 1949). At this level, we can recognize that scientists' decision to build a model of the Earth's climate, for example, reflects their judgement that studying this topic is a good and worthwhile pursuit. We can also recognize that the decision to build a model of the Earth's climate reflects the judgement that to do so is a *priority*: at least in some sense, it is more pressing or important than studying the climate on Mars (i.e., even if scientists would agree that studying the climate on Mars is also good and worthwhile, they accept the opportunity cost in this context and choose Earth over Mars). Furthermore, building a model of the Earth's climate reflects the judgement that doing so is *defensible*: that is, there are no ethical reasons *not* to model the Earth's climate, as there might be not to engage in certain other research practices (e.g., experimental testing on animals).

We can characterize the notion of 'values' in the loose and general way we do here, appealing to what's considered 'important' or 'worthwhile' or 'a priority' or 'defensible', or we can tighten the notion up with a more abstract framework coming from decision theory, defining 'values' in the way that decision theorists define 'preferences over prospects' – that is, in terms of what states of affairs in the world an agent prefers to have obtain over another. For example, to say that an agent thinks 'building a model of the Earth's climate is a good and worthwhile pursuit' means the agent prefers the state of affairs in a world where the model is built (and the time and money expended to do so) to the state of affairs in a world where the model is not built. To say that 'building a model of the Earth's climate is more pressing or important than studying the climate on Mars' means the agent prefers the state of affairs where a model of the Earth's climate exists and a model of Mars' climate doesn't, over the opposite state of affairs. To say that 'building a model of the Earth's climate is *defensible*' might mean something like 'a reasonably large number of reasonable people prefer the state of the world where the model exists to the one where it doesn't'. In what follows, we will sometimes use the more concrete language of the form 'X believes Y is a worthwhile project' or 'X thinks Y is more important than Z'. But it will also sometimes be more helpful to speak more abstractly in the language of decision theory of preferences over prospects.

In their discussion of big-picture 'what to represent' decisions in modelling, what Harvard et al. (2021) remind us is that not everyone supports building a scientific model for every purpose: any one of us might object to a model-building project if its goal were to highlight essential moral differences between men and women, for example (Kitcher 2010), or if its inevitable consequence would be to delay a time-sensitive Alpine rescue operation.

4.2.2 Fine-Grained Representational Decisions

But of course, we can zoom into 'what to represent' decisions in modelling with far more granularity than just looking at the research topic itself: when we say a model is 'of the Earth's climate', we typically mean that the model represents multiple attributes of that system in various different ways. What are some finer-grained 'what to represent' decisions? As we discussed in Section 1, models include both variables and parameters: crudely, a model's variables are the quantities it associates with a system that vary in space and time, while parameters are fixed quantities that help to specify the mathematical relationships between variables. For example, in a SEIR model, the value of R0 is a parameter, and the number of people infected at a given time is a variable.[9] Once we know a model's variables, we can talk about what the 'outcome' of a single run of a model is in terms of the final values that the variables take. And, last but not least, we can sometimes observe model-builders having the final values of certain variables as the outcomes of interest. The whole point of the of the model, from the point of view of the modellers, is to calculate the final value of these variables. We could call those the 'end points' of the model, but we should be aware that which outcomes count as end points is not a feature of the model: it is simply a fact about the model user. And a model that is built by one person with some set of end points in mind might end up being used by another user who picks a new and different set of outcomes as her end points.

Let's explore the question of the sense in which the finer-grained representational decisions concerning variables, parameters, and outcomes of interest (or 'end points') are value-laden. Recall that what we mean by value-laden here is that making these decisions will reflect not only the epistemic judgements of the

---

[9] However, you could also build an elaborate model in which the virus mutates and the value of R0 changes over time. This would turn R0 into a variable. If R0 is a variable, there will have to be causal input that determines the value it takes over time, showing that 'how to represent' decisions can quickly turn into 'what to represent' decisions.

agents making them, but their preferences over the possible prospects of making these decisions. To see why this is so, it is useful to think about how the modelling process typically goes. Upfront, there is usually a decision about which variables the final values of which are the end points of interest. In a climate model, for example, the global mean surface temperature of the Earth in some future decade, conditional on some emissions pathway, might be our end point of interest – or, it might be that researchers are interested in regional values of other variables, like precipitation or humidity. The fact that choosing an end point of *interest* is value-laden should be pretty obvious: people who think American agricultural production is especially *important* are apt to be especially *interested* in precipitation values in North America. To put this in the formal language of decision theory, if I prefer the prospect of having improved American agricultural production over the prospect of improved European agricultural production (of some given amount) then I might be more interested in a model whose primary end point is North American precipitation.

Once an end point is chosen, choosing which other variables and parameters to include is also value-laden, but in a more subtle way. The process goes like this: having chosen global mean surface temperature as our end point, we decide which other variables, and which parameters, are *causally relevant* in a model designed to project global mean surface temperature. This decision is value-laden both because it is dependent on the end points of interest, but also because whether, say, a particular variable will be considered to be 'causally relevant' might depend on the degree of accuracy to which we hope to forecast the value of the end point. And, of course, whether or not a forecast is considered 'accurate enough' is a value judgement too. Whether a climate model needs to include carbon sinks and sources, for example, might depend on how accurate we want the results of the model to be. If I prefer the prospect of having a model that's available sooner rather than later and is less costly to build, but which is slightly less accurate, then I might choose to omit carbon sinks and sources from the model. If I prefer the prospect of having a model that takes longer and is more costly to build, but will provide more accurate information, I might do the work of including carbon sinks and sources.

4.2.3 Inferential Decisions

As we discussed in Section 3, decisions in the modelling process include not only representational decisions but also *inferential decisions*. That is, at the stage of model interpretation, the goal is generally to use model results to infer facts about the world. This requires assessing the ethical consequences of endorsing a fact as true when it is actually false, of remaining silent, and so on; so it is a value-laden decision. Furthermore, many facts that we might decide to infer from model results will embed normative, that is, value-laden, presuppositions (Alexandrova 2017). Inferential decisions based on model results have a straightforward moral significance, particularly when these decisions will directly influence public policy.

4.3 The Ethical Significance of Including and Excluding Variables

Of course, no model is a perfectly accurate and comprehensive depiction of a target system: all models include some variables and omit others. If a model does not include certain variables, this could signify one of two things. First, it might signify that the model-builders deemed that the variable was neither ethically significant itself nor causally relevant to an ethically significant outcome. Second, it might signify that the model-builders determined that, regardless of whether the variable is ethically significant, it is not the job of the model in question to inform us about that variable, which is often perfectly reasonable and unavoidable. Determining what representational decisions say about model-builders and the outcomes they consider morally significant is a complex matter, and because it is seldom possible to hear their perspectives first-hand, some people might say that observers can only speculate. Nonetheless, it is at least important to consider the *ethical significance* of representational decisions in the context of how model-builders intend a model to guide policy. Ordinary climate models, for example, include neither the economic costs of mitigation nor the economic damage of climate change, whereas so-called integrated assessment models (IAMs) (see Winsberg 2018) do include these. We should not conclude from this that the developers of ordinary climate models do not deem the economic costs of mitigation nor the economic damage of climate change to be morally significant, but rather that they expect their model results to play a less direct role in policy-making (with knowledge of economic factors coming from another source) than do the builders of IAMs. On the other hand, when an IAM is being used to directly inform policy, it is perfectly reasonable to ask for a discussion to establish whether all of the ethically significant outcomes were included in the model (Winsberg (2018) and Frisch (2018) discuss the question of whether or not they do).

As we noted, 'what to represent' decisions are often informed by *how* or *whether* the representation of something can be achieved. For example, if there are no high-quality data on some aspect of a target system, this may be the reason it is not represented in a model. This raises the question: do practical barriers negate the social and ethical significance of building a model that omits certain aspects of a system? Following Harvard et al. (2021), we say the answer is no, for *at least* the following reasons: (1) modellers *could* use low-quality data or estimates in order to represent it; (2) modellers *could* decline to build the model on the grounds that there are no adequate data or estimates on an important aspect of the system, and the model results would be problematically incomplete without them. Deciding between these types of alternatives involves not only considering epistemic values, but weighing social and ethical values (cf. (Peschard and van Fraassen 2014; Harvard and Winsberg 2022)).

In their discussion of 'how to represent' decisions, Harvard et al. (2021) focus on the fact that representational decisions often centre around what *inputs* to use for values of parameters in the model: for example, what data sources should be used to model the rates of cloud formation in a climate model grid cell, or the probability of hospital admission if people in various age brackets are infected with a virus. Decisions around what inputs to use in a model can be challenging to make, particularly because different data sources generally have different limitations and higher degrees of adequacy for some purposes than others. In general, these decisions are value-laden because the choice to use one input over another will have an effect on model results. In other words, people with different views around whether it is worse to overestimate or underestimate the value of a variable, for example, will be inclined to use different inputs to populate a parameter that influences that variable, if there is a choice to be made between inputs.

4.4 The Expected Utility of Representational Decisions

To put this discussion in the language of decision theory, I might prefer the expected downstream prospects of making one representational choice over another. Why would that be? Suppose I think one representational choice has high probability of overestimating the danger of climate change and a low probability of underestimating it. And that I think the other available representational choice will be the opposite. I might pick the first choice because my expected utility for the first choice is higher. That is, the utility of overestimating multiplied by its probability on the first choice, plus (or minus) the utility of underestimating multiplied by its probability on the first choice, is higher than all of the above on the second choice.

There are two important things to note here. First, notice that in this slightly more formal presentation, we have moved to the general language of a representational choice, rather than the language of 'what inputs to use for a parameter'. This is because the point here is very general. Considerations like the above can kick in for all representational decisions, whether they be choices of what to represent, or how to represent – including what inputs to use, or what mathematical function to use, or anything of the sort. Second, in our formal presentation, we imagine that the person making the representational decision knows the probabilities and utilities exactly. But this will not generally be the case. In order for me to choose representation R1 over R2, I need only know that

$$U1 \times P1 + U2(1 - P1) > (U1 \times P2 + U2(1 - P2)$$

where U1 and U2 are the utilities I assign to overestimating and underestimating, respectively, and P1 and P2 are the probabilities of overestimating on R1 and R2.

Note that I needn't know in virtue of what exact values of P1, P2, U1, and U2 this obtains: I need only holistically grasp that the inequality obtains for whatever reason. As representational decisions get more and more complex, intermixing with other representational decisions, and as outcomes move from being binary to being continuous and multidimensional, it becomes more and more likely that model-builders are employing the kind of reasoning we explain here only in the most implicit sense. To ask modellers, then, to articulate all of the values and probabilities that drive their representational decisions would be impossible, in practice, to satisfy as a general requirement (we discuss this further in Section 4.7). The degree to which these considerations tend to be implicit and suppressed will be important to our discussion. We can call this claim, that model-builders can rarely articulate the full epistemic and normative considerations that underpin their representational decisions, the *inarticulability thesis* (cf. Parker and Winsberg 2018; Winsberg 2012, 2018).

Returning to the specific issue of making choices of parameter values: to be sure, modellers can often perform a sensitivity analysis in order to explore the effect of using different inputs for different parameters. However, this generally leaves a value-laden decision to be made around which inputs will be used for the 'main' (or base-case) analysis versus a sensitivity analysis (keeping in mind that the results of a main analysis may be the ones emphasized in reports to policy-makers and/or the media). It is also a value-laden decision whether model users are better served by a precise estimate or one that fully reflects the range of uncertainty that comes from our imperfect knowledge of parameter values. Finally, there are often limits to how many sensitivity analyses modellers can perform in a timely way.

4.5 Case Study: Imperial College London Model

4.5.1 Background

The ICL model, running on CovidSim, was developed by Neil Ferguson and his team and was based on an earlier influenza model (Ferguson et al. 2005, 2006, 2020). The primary purpose of the model was to project the impact of various

Label	Policy	Description
CI	Case isolation in the home	Symptomatic cases stay at home for 7 days, reducing non-household contacts by 75% for this period. Household contacts remain unchanged. Assume 70% of household comply with the policy.
HQ	Voluntary home quarantine	Following identification of a symptomatic case in the household, all household members remain at home for 14 days. Household contact rates double during this quarantine period, contacts in the community reduce by 75%. Assume 50% of household comply with the policy.
SDO	Social distancing of those over 70 years of age	Reduce contacts by 50% in workplaces, increase household contacts by 25% and reduce other contacts by 75%. Assume 75% compliance with policy.
SD	Social distancing of entire population	All households reduce contact outside household, school or workplace by 75%. School contact rates unchanged, workplace contact rates reduced by 25%. Household contact rates assumed to increase by 25%.
PC	Closure of schools and universities	Closure of all schools, 25% of universities remain open. Household contact rates for student families increase by 50% during closure. Contacts in the community increase by 25% during closure.

Figure 8 Summary of NPI interventions considered in Report 9.
Source: Ferguson et al. (2020, table 2, 6).

possible policy choices on Covid-19 deaths and demand for hospital beds, including intensive care unit (ICU) beds. Specifically, the report considers a variety of permutations from a set of possible policy choices (in addition to a potential 'do nothing' policy), consisting of the following elements, shown in Figure 8.

The subsets of these NPIs considered to be 'mitigation' strategies that the model explored were: PC; CI; CI&HQ; CI&SD; CI&HQ&SDO; and PC&CI&HQ&SDO. All of these strategies are 'shown' to result in massive overwhelm of the healthcare system, as shown in Figure 9.

'Suppression' is defined as being able to 'reduce R to close to 1 or below' (Ferguson et al. 2020, 10). The report cautions that, at least, '[c]ase isolation, general social distancing, and either school and university closure or home quarantine' are required to achieve suppression, but the only 'suppression' strategy whose simulation results are presented in the report is the combination of all four elements (i.e., '[h]ome isolation of cases, household quarantine, school and university closures, and social distancing of the entire population'). Ferguson et al. (2020) show the simulation results of instituting these policies cycling on and off for the 18 months they expected it to take to achieve a vaccine (assuming a baseline R_0 value of 2.2) (Figure 10).

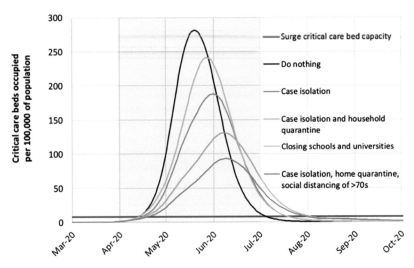

Figure 9 Report 9's projections for critical care (ICU) bed requirements under various mitigation and suppression strategies.

Source: Ferguson et al. (2020, 8).

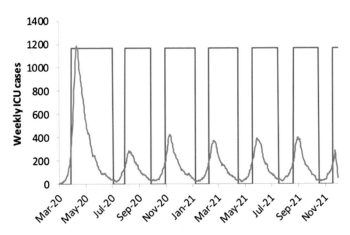

Figure 10 Adaptive triggering of suppression illustrated in Report 9.

Source: Ferguson et al. (2020, 12).

In building the model, the modellers aimed to steer policy choices by the UK Government, as well, to a lesser degree, as other governments around the world, by highlighting the extremely high death toll, and burden on healthcare systems, that would ensue from pursuing all but the last of those policy choices (Broadbent and Streicher 2022). Ferguson et al. (2020, 16) said:

We therefore conclude that epidemic suppression is the only viable strategy at the current time. The social and economic effects of the measures which are needed to achieve this policy goal will be profound. Many countries have adopted such measures already, but even those countries at an earlier stage of their epidemic (such as the United Kingdom) will need to do so imminently.

4.5.2 What Is Represented? Study Topic and End Points in Context

Following the basic framework outlined in Section 4.2, we can begin to outline some big-picture value judgements that went into building the ICL model. First and foremost, building this model reflects the judgement that it is an ethically defensible project: in other words, that it is desirable to seek more information about the likely effects of certain policy choices on Covid-19 deaths and hospitalizations. It is important to realize that this needn't be taken for granted. It is not hard to imagine people having a set of values according to which many of the policy choices explored in the model, particularly those that involved restrictions on various liberties, constitute violations of fundamental rights and should not even be considered. It is also not hard to imagine having a set of values, and a set of prior beliefs about the severity of the virus, on which it would have been morally unacceptable to delay action even long enough to carry out the modelling project – or to accept any risk at all that the model would erroneously steer policy-makers away from drastic suppression measures. It is only according to a certain set of values, and a certain set of prior beliefs given the state of evidence at the time, and a certain confidence that a minimally informative model could be built, that it would appear the right thing to build a model like the ICL model and to consider using its output to evaluate the costs and benefits of the kinds of policy choices that are explored in the model.

Next comes representational decisions concerning what the primary end points of the model ought to be. In the ICL model, the variables taken to be primary end points were Covid-19 infections, hospitalizations, occupancy of intensive care hospital beds due to Covid-19, and Covid-19 deaths. Including these as end points in a pandemic mitigation model signifies an ethical judgement that these are important outcomes to consider when reasoning about what NPIs to implement to help slow the pandemic. What about the outcomes that were excluded from the model? Recall that if a model does *not* include certain outcomes this could signify one of two things. The fact that the ICL model did not project the impact of the possible policy choices explored on things like educational outcomes and economic output could be interpreted in two ways: either as suggesting that these outcomes were not ethically significant, or as suggesting that decision-makers would have to look elsewhere to get this information.

This highlights the degree to which models must be understood in the context of the intended purposes of their users. It is *not built into the ICL model* whether it is intended to be a tactical model that can be used, directly, to assess different policy choices, or intended to be used alongside other sources of information about the effects these choices would have on things other than Covid-19 deaths, hospitalizations, and so on. But insofar as we can read the famous 'Report 9' (Ferguson et al. 2020), which was the primary document produced with the help of the ICL model, as a policy guidance document,[10] we can read it as suggesting that these outcomes were relatively ethically insignificant in comparison to the outcomes that were in fact part of the model.

Here is another way to frame the same point. If you happen to believe that policy choices that were guided with the help of a model were made without due consideration of a certain dimension of their consequences, it is difficult to assign moral responsibility for that moral failure. Responsibility could lie with the model-builders for failing to include those dimensions among their model end points, or it could lie with policy-makers for relying on only one kind of expertise (say, infectious disease epidemiology) when in fact two kinds of expertise (educational psychology as well as infectious disease epidemiology) were required. Or responsibility could fall on both parties. But in the case of Report 9, it seems clear that the ICL group judged that their model results alone could guide policy, and that their recommended strategy should be implemented *despite its social and economic effects*: 'We therefore conclude that epidemic suppression is the only viable strategy at the current time. The social and economic effects of the measures which are needed to achieve this policy goal will be profound' (Ferguson et al. 2020, 16).

4.5.3 Finer-Grained Representational Decisions

Other Variables

While representational decisions concerning what variables to include as end points in the ICL model (e.g., 'Should learning loss be an end point in the model?') have a particularly obvious ethical importance, decisions about what *other* variables to represent are value-laden too. One example is the decision to represent the ages of inhabitants of the United States and the United Kingdom, and their status as workers or students, but not their race, income, postal code, or occupation. As a result of this decision, the ICL model is not adequate for exploring research questions like: (1) whether a mitigation or suppression

---

[10] See Broadbent and Streicher (2022) for the view that Report 9 was intended to be an argument that the UK ought to adopt maximum suppression and that its cousin, Report 13, was intended as an argument that other nations, including developing nations, ought to do likewise.

strategy will lead to a racially unjust distribution of infections, hospitalizations, and deaths; or (2) whether such a strategy will differentially affect people of different professions. For example, will the closing of non-essential industries result in the burden of the disease falling primarily on those who provide essential services? As we noted in Section 1, at the heart of computational models like climate models and models of disease spread are the bits of math that jointly create the behaviour of the model, given its starting state, and the choice of counterfactual scenarios (from among all the infinite possible counterfactual scenarios) that it is designed to investigate. Usually, this requires picking other variables besides the ones being studied as end points, the mathematical relationships between them, and the values of parameters that feature in the equations that specify those relationships. The ICL model, for example, does not include among its variables the time of year and its possible impact on viral transmission. This makes it impossible for the model to explore the possibility that the virus could come in waves due to an underlying seasonality of the virus.

Parameters

Overall, the ICL model employed equations with almost 900 different parameters. Given its purpose, the model needed inputs for the expected Covid-19 death rate, hospitalization rate, and ICU admittance rate for every 100,000 people infected in each of several different age brackets, given in a table in Figure 11.

At the time that Report 9 came out, in the middle of March 2020, none of the correct values of these inputs were well known. (Indeed, our estimates of them at the time of writing now remain imperfect.) One moral judgement that could have been made at the time was that our confidence intervals around these input values were too large to make modelling the impact of different possible policy choices a worthwhile project. If, for example, one thought that the possible values for the infection fatality rate of SARS-CoV-2 at the time could be anywhere between 0.1% and 3%, and one thought, as the ICL team clearly did, that you had to pick a single value (at least relative to each age bracket) then you might think that a model of this kind would be useless for assessing the costs and benefits of policy choices. That's because you might think that it is fairly obvious that, if the infection fatality rate (IFR) is 0.1%, the most stringent strategies are almost certainly going to look too costly, and if it's 3%, they are almost certainly going to look like they are morally required. If you thought that, you might conclude that getting a better estimate of the numbers in Table 2 was a much higher priority than building a model like the ICL model – indeed, it might even be a condition on the moral permissibility of building it.

Age-group (years)	% symptomatic cases requiring hospitalisation	% hospitalised cases requiring critical care	Infection Fatality Ratio
0 to 9	0.1%	5.0%	0.002%
10 to 19	0.3%	5.0%	0.006%
20 to 29	1.2%	5.0%	0.03%
30 to 39	3.2%	5.0%	0.08%
40 to 49	4.9%	6.3%	0.15%
50 to 59	10.2%	12.2%	0.60%
60 to 69	16.6%	27.4%	2.2%
70 to 79	24.3%	43.2%	5.1%
80+	27.3%	70.9%	9.3%

Figure 11 Estimates of virus morbidity and fatality from Verity et al. (2020) used in Report 9.

Source: Ferguson et al. (2020, table 1, 5).

Note: The table is somewhat confusing because fatalities are given as a percentage of infections, but hospitalizations are given as a percentage of 'symptomatic infections', and ICU beds are given as a percentage of hospitalizations. If we dig into the code, we can determine that two-thirds of infections are expected to be symptomatic, and so the percentage of overall infections that will require hospitalization is 0.66 times the numbers in this column.

Since the ICL team obviously decided to proceed with the modelling project, how did they choose those values? In early March 2020, researchers had at least two sources of data available to them for the parameters in Ferguson et al. (2020, table 1) (Verity et al, 2020). The first was the Diamond Princess (DP) cruise ship. This was the first 'natural experiment' of a Covid-19 outbreak, where every single passenger had been tested for infection and the health outcomes of each passenger were well known. The second was the data available from the first 'epicentre' of the pandemic: Hubei province in China. The advantages and disadvantages of each data source were clear. The advantage of the DP data was that they were comprehensive. The exact number of infected people was known as was the exact number of each health outcome. The disadvantage was that the number of people was relatively small, and the age structure of the population was unusual. Most of the passengers were rather old and most of the crew were very young. There were very few intermediate-aged people in the data set. The advantage of the Hubei dataset was the mirror image of the disadvantages of the DP set. The dataset was large and every age demographic was included. The main disadvantage was that while the numerators for all of these outcomes were relatively well known,[11] the denominators

---

[11] We say 'relatively' because the ICL group gathered the data from newspaper reports, not from scientific sources.

were not known at all. That is, how many people had died of Covid-19 in Hubei and how many had been hospitalized was known, but it was not known how many infections this represented. Knowing the *ratios* of these numbers, however, was crucial to estimating the parameters needed for the ICL model.

The ICL group responded to this lacuna by looking at repatriation flights from Hubei into the United States and Europe. That is, at the time of the outbreak, citizens of the United States and some European countries were evacuated from Hubei province and returned to their home countries. Each person on these flights was carefully screened for infection with SARS-CoV-2. The ICL group used the proportion of expatriates who were infected to estimate the incidence of infection in Hubei at large. The disadvantages of these methods were obvious. For one thing, this ended up being a very small sample. In total, only six people were found to be infected on the flights.[12] Had, by chance, a seventh person tested positive, then all the values in Table 2 would have been six-sevenths the size they are. Another disadvantage was that the method assumed that very wealthy and culturally outlying expatriates had a degree of infection that was representative of the underlying population.

So the makers of the ICL model had at least two choices with regard to this 'how to represent' question: they could have generated something like Ferguson et al.'s (2020) Table 1 from the Hubei data or from the DP data. In what way did values influence this choice? The model-builders could clearly see that the IFR and hospitalization rates that came from the Hubei data were considerably higher than from the data from the DP.[13] Thus, choosing the Hubei data made it more likely the IFR would be overestimated than opting for the DP data, and less likely that it would be underestimated. Thus, the more serious you consider the harm of a Covid-19 death and/or hospitalization, and the less serious you regard the various harms of the mitigation and suppression strategies being considered, the more inclined you will be to choose the Hubei data, and perhaps the more inclined you will be to use the repatriation flight method for estimating the denominator than some other method that produced a lower IFR.

To return to a point we made in Section 4.4 that we called the *inarticulability thesis*, it is probably not reasonable for us to think that Ferguson and his

---

[12] 'In international Wuhan residents repatriated on six flights, we estimated a prevalence of infection of 0·87% (95% CI 0·32–1·9; six of 689)' (Verity et al, 2020, 675).

[13] Verity et al. (2020) use Ferguson et al.'s (2020) table 1 to estimate what the IFR on the DP would have been, given the age structure of the population, if table 1 were correct and this came to a value of 2.9%. The observed IFR on the ship, however, was 1.4%. This already shows that the estimates they were getting from Wuhan were higher than they would have got from the DP. But it actually understates the case because the hospitalization and death rates for the younger decades is more overestimated in Verity than it is for the older decades, and the way they do the comparison somewhat obscures this.

colleagues had in mind exact probabilities that the Hubei data were closer to reality than the DP data. Recall that what rationally guides representational decisions like the choice between the Hubei data and the DP data is utility maximization, and that is a function of the values we assign to the various states of affairs that might follow from our representational decisions being good or bad, along with the probabilities we assign to the various good and bad outcomes that could follow from particular representational decisions.

Suppose that the members of the ICL group had one, and only one, binary choice to make: use the DP data or the Hubei data. And suppose that they had in mind exact probability distributions that they assigned to each dataset overestimating and underestimating the effectiveness of each intervention to various degrees, say P(DP) and P(H). And suppose they had a complicated function of utilities over the space of each of those degrees of overestimation and underestimation. Even articulating just this amount of information would be overwhelming. But the situation is far worse than this: they have over 900 representational choices to make (just regarding the items they chose to represent, excluding those they chose to ignore!), and most of those choices are not in fact binary. They could, in principle, have had whole probability distributions over possible values of all the numbers in Ferguson et al.'s (2020) table 1. This suggests that, in fact, in a complex modelling situation like the one faced by the ICL team, a whole host of representational choices have to be made in conjunction with each other, with only a very coarse-grained and holistic assessment of the expected utility of a small subset of a nearly infinite set of possible choices they could have made. This is why the inarticulability thesis cautions that the decision could only have been made based on a rough expected utility estimation, without the modellers having precise values of probabilities and utilities in mind. Their choice of data set is ultimately the result of an inchoate mix of epistemic assessments and value commitments that cannot be fully articulated.

4.5.4 Uncertainty

Another 'how to represent' question concerns how to represent, in a model, our uncertainty regarding the best value of the relevant parameters. For example, the ICL model assumes that when people socially distance, their probability of getting infected at home increases by 25%. But why 25%? Why not 35%? In fact, there were no data or research to support any particular choice in the model, since we had few well-established rates for any past virus, let alone rates for the novel SARS-CoV-2 virus. It is very common in modelling to attempt to deal with uncertainty about the correct value of parameters by running a sensitivity analysis. The idea is to run the model on a wide sample of parameter values, in order to try to figure out how sensitive the model is to small differences in those values, and to try to figure out which values do the best job of capturing known data. In climate modelling, this is referred to as doing a 'perturbed physics ensemble'. But the ICL model was used to influence major policy decisions in the absence of any study of parameter sensitivity.

Fortunately, Edeling et al. (2021) finally undertook such a study in November 2020. They wrote:

> Here we report on parametric sensitivity analysis and uncertainty quantification of the code. From the 940 parameters used as input into CovidSim, we find a subset of 19 to which the code output is most sensitive – imperfect knowledge of these inputs is magnified in the outputs by up to 300%. The model displays substantial bias with respect to observed data, failing to describe validation data well. Quantifying parametric input uncertainty is therefore not sufficient: the effect of model structure and scenario uncertainty must also be properly understood. (Edeling et al. 2021, 128).

They found, in particular, that almost two-thirds of the differences in the model's results could be attributed to changes in just three especially important variables: the length of the latent period during which an infected person has no symptoms and can't pass the virus on; the effectiveness of social distancing; and how long after getting infected a person goes into isolation. More importantly, Edeling et al. (2021) found that for most values of these parameters, 5–6 times as many people die during 'suppression' than the model predicted using the values that the ICL group used. Thus, Edeling et al. (2021) show that, had Ferguson's group done a sensitivity analysis over the range of parameter values that were consistent with what was known about the virus, they would have been unable to show that the suppression strategy they appeared to be recommending would have had much benefit with respect to Covid-19 outcomes.

It is not hard to see that had Report 9 (Ferguson et al. 2020) included a sensitivity analysis of the kind found in Edeling et al. (2021), its influence on policy-makers and the public might have been less dramatic. After all, Edeling et al. (2021) seemed to show that it was consistent with what we knew in March 2020 that the mitigation and suppression strategies considered in Report 9 were all going to be equally ineffective. So we can see two ways in which the choice of how to represent these parameter values was value-laden. First, the ICL team chose values of parameters that maximized the projected benefits of the strategy they appeared to be recommending. Thus, they appear to be judging it to be less serious a mistake to overestimate the effectiveness of those strategies than to underestimate them.

Second, the choice not to include a sensitivity analysis in the characterization of the model output we find in the report was itself highly value-laden.

One possibility is that it reflected the value judgement that urgent action was required before there was time for the sensitivity analysis to be carried out. Another possibility is that it reflected the value judgement that an estimation of the degree of uncertainty regarding the effectiveness of the measures would be less valuable than the precise, fine-grained projection they in fact made. This is always a balance of values that model-builders and interpreters face: how to balance the benefit of the informativeness of a precise projection against the value of the confidence one can have in a wider, imprecise estimate of that same benefit (Winsberg 2018). Another possible explanation of the ICL group's failure to do a sensitivity analysis is that they deemed that doing so would be too likely to cause governments to wrongly choose to abstain from maximum suppression (i.e., by emphasizing the degree of existing uncertainty). This obviously would reflect a value judgement about how bad such an outcome would be.

4.5.5 Choice of Counterfactuals for Projection

Let's compare the way that the ICL model and climate models make projections. The ICL model projections are conditional on policy choices, while climate models are conditional on representative carbon pathways (RCPs). The latter are not policy choices: they are outcomes that are conditional on policy choices and numerous other factors acting in complex interaction with one another; there are no uncontroversial connections between policy choices and carbon pathways. In comparison, the ICL model takes policy choices as *counterfactuals for projection*. Model developers are thus put in the position of estimating how, for example, university and school closures will affect social contact rates – but there is enormous uncertainty around such relationships, not least because they stand to vary from setting to setting. Imagine putting climate modellers in a similar position: for example, asking climate modellers to assume that regulations imposed on nuclear power plant builders are reduced and subsidies are provided to electric utilities that build out solar power infrastructure. Our confidence in the model would have to be relatively low: the results would no longer reflect a causal pathway of which scientists have a good understanding (Harvard and Winsberg 2021). So the decision to represent possible policies in the model, rather than simply putting in contact rates that would be the *outcome* of policy choices, forced the modellers to choose how to represent those choices. This opens up a huge number of choices to make. And there was enormous uncertainty concerning nearly every one of these choices, many of which take the form of parameters built into the model's coding. Most modelling choices were relatively unconstrained by data or background knowledge; and when there was data, it was of poor quality.

4.6 Moral Responsibilities in Modelling

In this section, we have explored the consequences of the claim, developed in Section 3, that model-building involves a kind of epistemic risk that is fundamentally different from the kind of epistemic risk involved in endorsing a truth-apt claim as a fact. In particular, we used the example of the ICL computational model of Covid-19, called 'CovidSim', to highlight the ways in which making representational decisions – of what to represent and how to represent it – is highly value-laden.

One thing this discussion highlights is how the value-ladenness of modelling laces the practice of model-building and model-using with significant moral responsibilities. Model-builders and model users, especially model users who are policy-makers, face significant moral responsibilities because the choice to model at all, and the choices of how to model, can have serious moral consequences. Thus, model-builders and users are morally responsible for building the *right* models for the *right* purposes and for making representational choices that embody the *right* balance of risks (i.e., that their models will fail to be adequate for purpose in one way rather than another).

But, of course, every use of the word 'right' in the previous sentence will be highly value-dependent. And when model-builders and model users are working, as they so often do, on behalf of the public, the question of what constitutes the *right* set of values for informing the modelling process can become overwhelmingly vexed. How can model-builders and model users possibly navigate these incredibly turbulent waters? How can they ensure they are not imposing their idiosyncratic values on the public?

One proposal that we find in the general 'values in science' literature is that scientists should strive to make their own reasonable methodological decisions and then be transparent about what values guided those decisions (Douglas 2009; Elliott 2017; Elliott and McKaughan 2014; Schroeder 2017). There are two considerations here that suggest this is unlikely to do the work it needs to do – to avoid imposing idiosyncratic values on the public. For example, the ICL group (see Verity et al. 2020) are relatively 'transparent' about the fact that they chose the Hubei data set over the DP data set. (As we saw, Verity et al. (2020) showed that the estimate of IFR from Hubei was at least twice as large as the one you would get from the DP, and they chose to use the former exclusively.) But for 'transparency' to mitigate the problems discussed here, it should enable members of the public to figure out whether the choice the ICL group made is or isn't the one *they would have made*, given their values. If the public can see that they would have made the same choice, then no idiosyncratic values risk being involved. If they can't tell that, then the strong possibility exists that the ICL group is being value-laden in a way that the public would fundamentally object to, and that this fact remains hidden. Therefore, it is a criterion of success for the transparency proposal, that transparency leads to members of the public being able to tell if modellers are making choices that fail to accord with their values. We can call this the 'congruence' criterion.

In the kinds of modelling projects we are looking at here, that is, complex models that incorporate diverse sources of evidence and aim to directly inform policy, it seems unclear whether the congruency criterion could be met. Indeed, the inarticulability thesis seems strongly to suggest otherwise. The inarticulability thesis, recall, says that it is unrealistic to ask modellers to articulate all of the values and probabilities that drive their representational choices. In principle, how could modellers say more than 'We chose the Hubei data over the DP data', in a way that would satisfy the congruence criterion? What the literature seems to suggest is that modellers should issue transparent statements in a form such as, 'We chose the data set that erred on the side of overestimating the risk of death from Covid-19' (e.g., Douglas 2009). In principle, this sort of statement could be adequate for satisfying the congruence criterion. However, notice that it is only adequate if what modellers mean by it is that 'no matter how high a risk estimate a data set would yield, and regardless of our assessment of the quality or accuracy of a dataset, we would always pick the data set that erred on the side of overestimating the risk of death from Covid-19' and if members of the public share this extreme view. Otherwise, a statement of this type does not allow members of the public to determine whether they would have acted as the modellers did, because it doesn't tell them the ICL group's *relative* weighting of different harms. It doesn't, crucially, tell a member of the public how much more the ICL group values avoiding a Covid-19 death than they do a job loss, or a child losing a year of education. And unless members of the public know this, they can't be sure whether they would have chosen the data set that produced a higher death rate, irrespective of how high that death rate is and how likely that data set was to be the better one. Unless the ICL group can tell members of the public what *all* their value commitments are, in a fine-grained form like 'We think avoiding one Covid-19 death is worth losing 100 child learning years' for every single relevant policy consequence, then members of the public won't be able to tell whether the ICL group made the same representational decisions they would have. And the inarticulability thesis suggests it is not feasible for transparency to take this form.

Instead of merely asking for transparency, we could ask that scientists simply make the choices that reflect the 'right' values (Schroeder 2017). But what would this mean? Roughly speaking, there are two things we could mean by the 'right' purposes and the 'right' balances of risks. 'Right' here could mean the ethically correct ones, or it could mean the ones that are actually held by the public (Schroeder 2017). Arguably, not being the ethically *wrong* purposes and balance of risks is a minimal condition on being the satisfactory ones. A model that assumes men's health outcomes are more important than women's is not an ethically defensible model. But, also arguably, not being ethically wrong is not a narrow enough constraint on representational choices in a model. There might have been, for example, a value commitment about the relative value of preventing Covid-19 deaths versus preventing job losses, and all their attendant harms, on which choosing the Hubei data set was the right choice, and another value commitment in relation to the same consequences on which the DP data set would have been the right choice. And it might very well have been the case that reasonable people would disagree about which was the right set of values to have. If that's right, then having scientists limit themselves to ethically permissible representational choices will underdetermine those choices and leave them open to making choices that do not reflect the values of the majority of the people on whose behalf decision-makers will be acting when they make use of the model.

4.7 Public Participation in Modelling

In modelling projects that aim to directly inform public policy, it seems to us that scientists have an obligation to make the 'right' choices in the sense of 'right' that means 'in accord with publicly held values'. Something like this line of argument is defended by Alexandrova and Fabian (2021) with respect to decisions regarding which 'thick concepts' to employ in science. Their idea is that if scientists are going to theorize about something like 'well-being', they need to use a concept of well-being that accords with the public's. Here, we are in broad agreement with them: in fact, we think their basic idea needs to be extended far more widely to include representational decisions in modelling generally. To ensure that thick concepts in science reflect public values, Alexandrova and Fabian (2021) propose a process of 'co-production', whereby scientists and members of the public work together to determine how to construct relevant measures such as 'well-being'. A similar process of co-production to build policy-relevant models seems like a fruitful one to explore, and in fact various research groups across disciplines have endeavoured to involve members of the public in *participatory modelling projects* (Bunka et al. 2022; Gray et al. 2016; Staniszewska et al. 2021; Voinov and Bousquet 2010; Xie et al. 2021). Currently, it is unclear whether participatory modelling projects are meeting the goal of ensuring that models reflect public values, and various challenges with this type of co-production will have to be addressed in future research. Among various challenges are the idea that co-production could become a 'box-checking' exercise (Alexandrova and Fabian 2021), that members of the public won't be able to understand what's going on in the modelling process, or that modellers won't be able to articulate the relevant considerations that would link their values to representational choices.

Prima facie, it seems like asking the public to co-produce a model is a bigger ask than co-producing a thick concept like well-being. For example, asking members of the public to weigh in on what aspects of well-being are most important to them (e.g., having a feeling of purpose in life) requires much less technical understanding than does expecting them to recognize that shortening the latency period of a virus will make NPIs look more effective than lengthening it and therefore implicitly weights as more serious the risk of allowing too many Covid-19 deaths than the risk of unduly damaging the economy, and by how much. Or figuring out that one version of a sensitivity analysis privileges precision over confidence, and by how much. What seems to be required are normative guidelines for public modelling projects that articulate how representational decisions should be made collaboratively between modellers and stakeholders (Harvard and Winsberg 2023; Husereau et al. 2022). In addition to this, one might think that normative guidelines are required not only with respect to how representational decisions should be made, but with respect to how those decisions should be *implemented in code* when the representations in question are complex computational models. Indeed, this is the focus of Horner and Symons (2020), who point to the concrete challenges involved in software engineering and the various potential errors that can result from this aspect of modelling practice (cf. Primiero 2014). Horner and Symons (2020) argue that software engineering standards, too, are negotiable matters that should involve public deliberation concerning trade-offs (e.g., regarding safety, uncertainty, urgency, resources, risk, etc.). As representational decisions intersect with numerous other socially significant decisions throughout the modelling process (What software should modellers use? Should all models for public decision-making be 'open source'? How should such models be validated?), an important initial question concerns the appropriate *scope* for public participation in modelling and corresponding normative guidelines. More philosophical and empirical work is required to conceptualize and address these questions.

4.8 Conclusion

In this section we used 'CovidSim' as an example to illustrate the ways in which representational choices in modelling, and the stage of model interpretation at which facts are endorsed, both involve values, and we argued that this places moral responsibilities on model-builders, model interpreters, and the policy-makers who engage with them. Regarding model-builders, we canvassed three different ways in which they can discharge their responsibilities: by being transparent about their values, by using ethically correct values, or by appealing to publicly held values. We highlighted the respects in which the third way seems to be the only fully satisfactory one of the three, but also by far the most difficult to achieve.

References

Abramowitz, Gab, Nadja Herger, Ethan Gutmann, et al. 2019. 'ESD Reviews: Model Dependence in Multi-Model Climate Ensembles: Weighting, Sub-Selection and Out-of-Sample Testing'. *Earth System Dynamics* 10 (1): 91–105.

Alexandrova, Anna. 2017. *A Philosophy for the Science of Well-Being*. Oxford: Oxford University Press.

Alexandrova, Anna, and Mark Fabian. 2021. 'Democratising Measurement: Or Why Thick Concepts Call for Coproduction'. *European Journal for Philosophy of Science* 12 (1): 1–23. https://doi.org/10.1007/s13194-021-00437-7.

Alvich, Jason. n.d.-a. 'Earth System (ESM4)'. Accessed 18 November 2022. www.gfdl.noaa.gov/earth-system-esm4/.

Alvich, Jason. n.d.-b. 'Model Development'. Accessed 18 November 2022. www.gfdl.noaa.gov/model-development/.

Ankeny, Rachel, and Sabina Leonelli. 2021. *Model Organisms*. Cambridge: Cambridge University Press.

Bailer-Jones, Daniela M. 2002. 'Scientists' Thoughts on Scientific Models'. *Perspectives on Science* 10 (3): 275–301. https://doi.org/10.1162/106361402321899069.

    2009. *Scientific Models in Philosophy of Science*. Pittsburgh, PA: University of Pittsburgh Press.

Bailer-Jones, Daniela M., and Coryn A. L. Bailer-Jones. 2002. 'Modeling Data: Analogies in Neural Networks, Simulated Annealing and Genetic Algorithms'. *Magnani and Nersessian* 2002: 147–65. https://doi.org/10.1007/978-1-4615-0605-8_9.

Basshuysen, Philippe van, Lucie White, Donal Khosrowi, and Mathias Frisch. 2021. 'Three Ways in Which Pandemic Models May Perform a Pandemic'. *Erasmus Journal for Philosophy and Economics* 14 (1): 110–27. https://doi.org/10.23941/ejpe.v14i1.582.

Bergstrom, Carl T. @CT_Bergstrom. 19 April 2020. 'I Believe That If #SARS-CoV-2 Is Allowed to Spread ...'. Twitter Page. https://twitter.com/CT_Bergstrom/status/1252075528711860224.

Bergstrom, Carl, and Natalie Dean. 2020. 'What the Proponets of "Natural" Herd Immunity Don't Say: Try to Reach It without a Vaccine, and Millions will Die'. *New York Times*, 1 May 2020. www.nytimes.com/2020/05/01/opinion/sunday/coronavirus-herd-immunity.html.

Biggs, Adam T., and Lanny F. Littlejohn. 2021. 'Revisiting the Initial COVID-19 Pandemic Projections'. *The Lancet Microbe* 2 (3): e91–2. https://doi.org/10.1016/S2666-5247(21)00029-X.

Black, Max. 1962. *Models and Metaphors: Studies in Language and Philosophy*. Ithaca, NY: Cornell University Press.

Bokulich, Alisa. 2011. 'How Scientific Models Can Explain'. *Synthese* 180 (1): 33–45. https://doi.org/10.1007/s11229-009-9565-1.

Bokulich, Alisa, and Wendy Parker. 2021. 'Data Models, Representation and Adequacy-for-Purpose'. *European Journal for Philosophy of Science* 11 (1): 1–26.

Briggs, Andrew, Mark Sculpher, and Karl Claxton. 2006. *Decision Modelling for Health Economic Evaluation*. Oxford: Oxford University Press.

Britton, Tom. 2010. 'Stochastic Epidemic Models: A Survey'. *Mathematical Biosciences* 225 (1): 24–35. https://doi.org/10.1016/j.mbs.2010.01.006.

Britton, Tom, Frank Ball, and Pieter Trapman. 2020. 'A Mathematical Model Reveals the Influence of Population Heterogeneity on Herd Immunity to SARS-CoV-2'. *Science* 369 (6505): 846–9. https://doi.org/10.1126/science.abc6810.

Broadbent, Alex. 2020. 'Lockdown Is Wrong for Africa'. *Mail & Guardian*, 8 April 2020. https://mg.co.za/article/2020-04-08-is-lockdown-wrong-for-africa/.

Broadbent, Alex, and Pieter Streicher. 2022. 'Can You Lock Down in a Slum? And Who Would Benefit If You Tried? Difficult Questions about Epidemiology's Commitment to Global Health Inequalities during Covid-19'. *Global Epidemiology* 4 (December): 100074. https://doi.org/10.1016/j.gloepi.2022.100074.

Bunka, Mary, Shahzad Ghanbarian, Linda Riches, et al. 2022. 'Collaborating with Patient Partners to Model Clinical Care Pathways in Major Depressive Disorder: The Benefits of Mixing Evidence and Lived Experience'. *Pharmacoeconomics* 40 (10): 971–7. https://doi.org/10.1007/s40273-022-01175-1.

Cartwright, Nancy. 1983. *How the Laws of Physics Lie*. Vol. 34. Oxford: Clarendon Press.

    1989. *Nature's Capacities and Their Measurement*. Oxford: Oxford University Press.

    2019. *Nature, the Artful Modeler: Lectures on Laws, Science, How Nature Arranges the World and How We Can Arrange It Better*. Vol. 23. Chicago, IL: Open Court Publishing.

Chikina, Maria, and Wesley Pegden. 2020. 'Modeling Strict Age-Targeted Mitigation Strategies for COVID-19'. *PLoS ONE* 15 (7): e0236237. https://doi.org/10.1371/journal.pone.0236237.

Choi, Yeon-Woo, Alexandre Tuel, and Elfatih A. B. Eltahir. 2021. 'On the Environmental Determinants of COVID-19 Seasonality'. *GeoHealth* 5 (6): e2021GH000413. https://doi.org/10.1029/2021GH000413.

Covid-19 Forecasting Team. 2022. 'Variation in the COVID-19 Infection–Fatality Ratio by Age, Time, and Geography during the Pre-Vaccine Era: A Systematic Analysis'. *The Lancet* 399 (10334): 1469–88. https://doi.org/10.1016/S0140-6736(21)02867-1.

Douglas, Heather. 2000. 'Inductive Risk and Values in Science'. *Philosophy of Science* 67 (4): 559–79.

2009. *Science, Policy, and the Value-Free Ideal*. Pittsburgh, PA: University of Pittsburgh Press. https://bit.ly/45lqr7P.

Downes, Stephen M. 1992. 'The Importance of Models in Theorizing: A Deflationary Semantic View'. *PSA: Proceedings of the Biennial Meeting of the Philosophy of Science Association* 1992 (1): 142–53. https://doi.org/10.1086/psaprocbienmeetp.1992.1.192750.

Edeling, Wouter, Hamid Arabnejad, Robbie Sinclair, et al. 2021. 'The Impact of Uncertainty on Predictions of the CovidSim Epidemiological Code'. *Nature Computational Science* 1 (2): 128–35. https://doi.org/10.1038/s43588-021-00028-9.

Elliott, Kevin Christopher. 2017. *A Tapestry of Values: An Introduction to Values in Science*. New York: Oxford University Press.

Elliott, Kevin C., and Daniel J. McKaughan. 2014. 'Nonepistemic Values and the Multiple Goals of Science'. *Philosophy of Science* 81 (1): 1–21.

Elliott, Kevin Christopher, and Ted Richards. 2017. *Exploring Inductive Risk: Case Studies of Values in Science*. New York: Oxford University Press.

Ferguson, Neil M., Derek A. T. Cummings, Simon Cauchemez, et al. 2005. 'Strategies for Containing an Emerging Influenza Pandemic in Southeast Asia'. *Nature* 437 (7056): 209–14.

Ferguson, Neil M., Derek A. T. Cummings, Christophe Fraser, et al. 2006. 'Strategies for Mitigating an Influenza Pandemic'. *Nature* 442 (7101): 448–52.

Ferguson, Neil, Daniel Laydon, Gemma Nedjati Gilani, et al. 2020. 'Report 9: Impact of Non-Pharmaceutical Interventions (NPIs) to Reduce COVID19 Mortality and Healthcare Demand'. Imperial College London. https://doi.org/10.25561/77482.

FitzGerald, J. Mark, Sofie Arnetorp, Caitlin Smare, et al. 2020. 'The Cost-Effectiveness of As-Needed Budesonide/Formoterol versus Low-Dose

Inhaled Corticosteroid Maintenance Therapy in Patients with Mild Asthma in the UK'. *Respiratory Medicine* 171: 106079. http://doi.org/10.1016/j .rmed.2020.106079.

Frigg, Roman, and Stephan Hartmann. 2012. 'Models in Science'. In *Stanford Encyclopedia of Philosophy*, edited by Edward N. Zalta. http://plato.stan ford.edu/archives/fall2012/entries/models-science.

Frigg, Roman, and James Nguyen. 2021. 'Seven Myths about the Fiction View of Models'. In *Models and Idealizations in Science*, edited by Alejandro Cassini and Juan Redmond, 133–57. Cham: Springer.

Frisch, Mathias. 2018. 'Modeling Climate Policies: The Social Cost of Carbon and Uncertainties in Climate Predictions'. In *Climate Modelling: Philosophical and Conceptual Issues*, edited by Elisabeth A. Lloyd and Eric Winsberg, 413–48. Cham: Springer. https://doi.org/10.1007/978-3-319-65058-6_14.

Giere, Ronald N. 1988. *Explaining Science: A Cognitive Approach*. Chicago, IL: University of Chicago Press.

1999. *Science without Laws*. Chicago, IL: University of Chicago Press.

2006. *Scientific Perspectivism*. Chicago, IL: University of Chicago Press.

Giere, Ronald N, John Bickle, and Robert F Mauldin. 1979. *Understanding Scientific Reasoning*. Belmont, CA : Thomson/Wadsworth.

Godfrey-Smith, Peter. 2009. 'Abstractions, Idealizations, and Evolutionary Biology'. In *Mapping the Future of Biology: Evolving Concepts and Theories*, edited by Anouk Barberousse, Michel Morange, and Thomas Pradeu. Boston Studies in the Philosophy of Science 266. Dordrecht: Springer Netherlands, 47–55. https://doi.org/10.1007/978-1-4020-9636-5_4.

Gray, Steven, Michael Paolisso, Rebecca Jordan, and Stefan Gray, eds. 2016. *Environmental Modeling with Stakeholders: Theory, Methods, and Applications*. Cham: Springer.

Handel, Andreas, Ira M Longini, and Rustom Antia. 2007. 'What Is the Best Control Strategy for Multiple Infectious Disease Outbreaks?'. *Proceedings of the Royal Society B: Biological Sciences* 274 (1611): 833–7. https://doi.org/10.1098/rspb.2006.0015.

Hartmann, Stephan. 1995. 'Models as a Tool for Theory Construction: Some Strategies of Preliminary Physics'. In *Theories and Models in Scientific Processes*, edited by William Herfel, Władysław Krajewski, Ilkka Niiniluoto, and Ryszard Wójcicki, 49–67. Amsterdam: Rodopi.

1998. 'Idealization in Quantum Field Theory'. In *Idealization IX: Idealization in Contemporary Physics*, edited by Niall Shanks, 99–122. Amsterdam: Rodopi.

Harvard, Stephanie, and Eric Winsberg. 2021. 'Causal Inference, Moral Intuition, and Modeling in a Pandemic'. *Philosophy of Medicine* 2 (2): 1–10.

2022. 'The Epistemic Risk in Representation'. *Kennedy Institute of Ethics Journal* 32 (1): 1–31.

2023. 'Patient and Public Involvement in Health Economics Modelling Raises the Need for Normative Guidance'. *Pharmacoeconomics* 41 (7): 733–40.

Harvard, Stephanie, Eric Winsberg, John Symons, and Amin Adibi. 2021. 'Value Judgments in a COVID-19 Vaccination Model: A Case Study in the Need for Public Involvement in Health-Oriented Modelling'. *Social Science & Medicine* 286. http://doi.org/10.1016/j.socscimed.2021.114323.

Hempel, Carl G. 1954. 'A Logical Appraisal of Operationism'. *Scientific Monthly* 79 (4): 215–20.

Hesse, Mary. 1963. *Models and Analogies in Science*. London: Sheed and Ward.

1967. 'Models and Analogy in Science'. In *Encyclopedia of Philosophy*, edited by Paul Edwards, 354–9. New York: Macmillan.

1974. *The Structure of Scientific Inference*. London: Macmillan.

Horner, Jack K., and John F. Symons. 2020. 'Software Engineering Standards for Epidemiological Models'. *History and Philosophy of the Life Sciences* 42 (4): 1–24.

Hughes, Richard I. G. 1997. 'Models and Representation'. *Philosophy of Science* 64 (S4): S325–36.

Husereau, Don, Michael Drummond, Federico Augustovski, et al. 2022. 'Consolidated Health Economic Evaluation Reporting Standards 2022 (CHEERS 2022) Statement: Updated Reporting Guidance for Health Economic Evaluations'. *Pharmacoeconomics* 40 (6): 601–9. https://doi.org/10.1007/s40273-021-01112-8.

Ioannidis, John P. A., Sally Cripps, and Martin A. Tanner. 2022. 'Forecasting for COVID-19 Has Failed'. *International Journal of Forecasting* 38 (2): 423–38. https://doi.org/10.1016/j.ijforecast.2020.08.004.

Jones, Martin R. 2005. 'Idealization and Abstraction: A Framework'. In *Idealization XII: Correcting the Model*, edited by Martin R. Jones and Nancy Cartwright, 173–217. Amsterdam: Rodopi.

Kitcher, Philip. 2010. 'Varieties of Freedom and Their Distribution'. *Social Research* 77 (3): 857–72.

Knutti, Reto. 2018. 'Climate Model Confirmation: From Philosophy to Predicting Climate in the Real World'. In *Climate Modelling: Philosophical and Conceptual Issues*, edited by Elisabeth A. Lloyd and Eric Winsberg, 325–59. Cham: Springer.

Knuuttila, Tarja. 2005. 'Models, Representation, and Mediation'. *Philosophy of Science* 72 (5): 1260–71. http://doi.org/doi:10.1086/508124.

——— 2011. 'Modelling and Representing: An Artefactual Approach to Model-Based Representation'. *Studies in History and Philosophy of Science Part A*, 42 (2): 262–71. http://doi.org/10.1016/j.shpsa.2010.11.034.

Laymon, Ronald. 1982. 'Scientific Realism and the Hierarchical Counterfactual Path from Data to Theory'. *PSA: Proceedings of the Biennial Meeting of the Philosophy of Science Association* 1982 (1): 107–21. https://doi.org/10.1086/psaprocbienmeetp.1982.1.192660.

——— 1985. 'Idealizations and the Testing of Theories by Experimentation'. In *Observation, Experiment, and Hypothesis in Modern Physical Science*, edited by Peter Achinstein and Owen Hannaway, 147–73. Cambridge, MA: MIT Press.

Leonelli, Sabina. 2010. 'Packaging Small Facts for Re-Use: Databases in Model Organism Biology'. In *How Well Do Facts Travel? The Dissemination of Reliable Knowledge*, edited by Peter Howlett and Mary S. Morgan, 325–48. Cambridge: Cambridge University Press. https://doi.org/10.1017/CBO9780511762154.017.

——— 2016. *Data-Centric Biology: A Philosophical Study*. Chicago, IL: University of Chicago Press.

——— 2019. 'What Distinguishes Data from Models?'. *European Journal for Philosophy of Science* 9 (2): 22. https://doi.org/10.1007/s13194-018-0246-0.

Levy, Arnon, and Adrian Currie. 2015. 'Model Organisms Are Not (Theoretical) Models'. *British Journal for the Philosophy of Science* 66 (2): 327–48. https://doi.org/10.1093/bjps/axt055.

Longino, Helen E. 1990. *Science as Social Knowledge: Values and Objectivity in Scientific Inquiry*. Princeton, NJ: Princeton University Press. https://bit.ly/48Km49q.

Magnani, Lorenzo, and Nancy J. Nersessian, eds. 2002. *Model Based Reasoning: Science, Technology, Values*. New York: Springer. https://doi.org/10.1007/978-1-4615-0605-8.

Magnani, Lorenzo, Nancy J. Nersessian, and Paul Thagard, eds. 1999. *Model-Based Reasoning in Scientific Discovery*. Boston, MA: Springer US. https://doi.org/10.1007/978-1-4615-4813-3.

Massimi, Michela. 2018a. 'Four Kinds of Perspectival Truth'. *Philosophy and Phenomenological Research* 96 (2): 342–59. https://doi.org/10.1111/phpr.12300.

——— 2018b. 'Perspectival Modeling'. *Philosophy of Science* 85 (3): 335–59. https://doi.org/10.1086/697745.

Mauritsen, Thorsten, Bjorn Stevens, Erich Roeckner, et al. 2012. 'Tuning the Climate of a Global Model'. *Journal of Advances in Modeling Earth Systems* 4 (3). http://onlinelibrary.wiley.com/doi/10.1029/2012MS000 154/full.

Mayo, Deborah. 1996. *Error and the Growth of Experimental Knowledge.* Chicago, IL: University of Chicago Press.

———. 2018. *Statistical Inference as Severe Testing: How to Get Beyond the Statistics Wars.* Cambridge: Cambridge University Press. https://doi.org/10.1017/9781107286184.

McMullin, Ernan. 1985. 'Galilean Idealization'. *Studies in History and Philosophy of Science Part A* 16 (3): 247–73. https://doi.org/10.1016/0039-3681(85)90003-2.

Morgan, Mary S., and Margaret Morrison, eds. 1999. *Models as Mediators: Perspectives on Natural and Social Science.* Cambridge: Cambridge University Press.

Morrison, Margaret. 1999. 'Models as Autonomous Agents'. In *Models as Mediators: Perspectives on Natural and Social Science*, edited by Mary S. Morgan and Margaret Morrison. Cambridge: Cambridge University Press, 38–65. https://doi.org/10.1017/CBO9780511660108.004.

———. 2000. *Unifying Scientific Theories: Physical Concepts and Mathematical Structures.* Cambridge: Cambridge University Press. https://doi.org/10.1017/CBO9780511527333.

———. 2005. 'Approximating the Real: The Role of Idealizations in Physical Theory'. In *Idealization XII: Correcting the Model*, edited by Martin R. Jones and Nancy Cartwright, 145–72. Amsterdam: Rodopi. https://doi.org/10.1163/9789401202732_009.

———. 2009. 'Understanding in Physics and Biology: From the Abstract to the Concrete'. In *Scientific Understanding: Philosophical Perspectives*, edited by Kai Eigner, Sabina Leonelli, and Henk W. de Regt, 123–45. Pittsburgh, PA: University of Pittsburgh Press.

Nersessian, Nancy J. 2010. *Creating Scientific Concepts.* Cambridge, MA: MIT Press.

Parker, Wendy. 2018. 'Climate Science'. In *Stanford Encyclopedia of Philosophy* (Fall 2023 Edition), edited by Edward N. Zalta and Uri Nodelman. https://plato.stanford.edu/entries/climate-science/.

Parker, Wendy S., and Eric Winsberg. 2018. 'Values and Evidence: How Models Make a Difference'. *European Journal for Philosophy of Science* 8 (1): 125–42.

Peschard, Isabelle. 2011. 'Making Sense of Modeling: Beyond Representation'. *European Journal for Philosophy of Science* 1 (3): 335–52. http://doi.org/10.1007/s13194-011-0032-8.

Peschard, Isabelle F., and Bas C. van Fraassen. 2014. 'Making the Abstract Concrete: The Role of Norms and Values in Experimental Modeling'. *Studies in History and Philosophy of Science Part A* 46: 3–10.

Primiero, Giuseppe. 2014. 'On the Ontology of the Computing Process and the Epistemology of the Computed'. *Philosophy and Technology* 27 (3): 485–9.

Redhead, Michael. 1980. 'Models in Physics'. *British Journal for the Philosophy of Science* 31 (2): 145–63.

Rucinski, Stefanea L., Matthew J. Binnicker, Amber S. Thomas, and Robin Patel. 2020. 'Seasonality of Coronavirus 229E, HKU1, NL63, and OC43 From 2014 to 2020'. *Mayo Clinic Proceedings* 95 (8): 1701–3. https://doi.org/10.1016/j.mayocp.2020.05.032.

Saatsi, Juha. 2016. 'Models, Idealisations, and Realism'. In *Models and Inferences in Science*, edited by Emiliano Ippoliti, Fabio Sterpetti, and Thomas Nickles, 173–89. Cham: Springer. https://doi.org/10.1007/978-3-319-28163-6_10.

Schroeder, S. A. 2017. 'Using Democratic Values in Science: An Objection and (Partial) Response'. *Philosophy of Science* 84 (5):1044–54.

Shanker, Roshni, and Prabhat Raghavan. 2021. 'The Invisible Crisis: Refugees and COVID-19 in India'. *International Journal of Refugee Law* 32 (4): 680–4. https://doi.org/10.1093/ijrl/eeab011.

Smeenk, Chris. 2020. 'Some Reflections on the Structure of Cosmological Knowledge'. *Studies in History and Philosophy of Science Part B: Studies in History and Philosophy of Modern Physics* 71: 220–31.

Staniszewska, Sophie, Edward M. Hill, Richard Grant, et al. 2021. 'Developing a Framework for Public Involvement in Mathematical and Economic Modelling: Bringing New Dynamism to Vaccination Policy Recommendations'. *Patient* 14 (4): 435–45. https://doi.org/10.1007/s40271-020-00476-x.

Sterrett, Susan G. 2006. 'Models of Machines and Models of Phenomena'. *International Studies in the Philosophy of Science* 20 (1): 69–80. https://doi.org/10.1080/02698590600641024.

2021. 'Scale Modeling'. In *Routledge Handbook of Philosophy of Engineering*, edited by Diane Michelfelder and Neelke Doorn, 394–407. New York: Routledge.

Stone, Dáithí A, and Reto Knutti. 2010. 'Weather and Climate'. In *Modelling the Impact of Climate Change on Water Resources*, edited by Fai Fung, Ana Lopez, and Mark New, 4–33. Chichester: Wiley-Blackwell.

Suppe, Frederick. 1972. 'What's Wrong with the Received View on the Structure of Scientific Theories?'. *Philosophy of Science* 39 (1): 1–19.

Suppes, Patrick. 1960. 'A Comparison of the Meaning and Uses of Models in Mathematics and the Empirical Sciences'. *Synthese* 12 (2–3): 287–301. https://doi.org/10.1007/BF00485107.

1962. 'Models of Data'. In *Logic, Methodology and Philosophy of Science: Proceedings of the 1960 International Congress*, edited by Ernest Nagel, Patrick Suppes, and Alfred Tarski, 252–61. Stanford, CA: Stanford University Press.

1969. 'Models of Data'. In *Studies in the Methodology and Foundations of Science*, 24–35. Dordrecht: Springer. http://link.springer.com/chapter/10.1007/978-94-017-3173-7_2.

2007. 'Statistical Concepts in Philosophy of Science'. *Synthese* 154 (3): 485–96. https://doi.org/10.1007/s11229-006-9122-0.

Teller, Paul. 2018. 'Referential and Perspectival Realism'. *Spontaneous Generations: A Journal for the History and Philosophy of Science* 9 (1): 151–64. https://doi.org/10.4245/sponge.v9i1.26990.

van Fraassen, Bas C. 1980. *The Scientific Image*. New York: Oxford University Press.

Verity, Robert, Lucy C. Okell, Ilaria Dorigatti, et al. 2020. 'Estimates of the Severity of Coronavirus Disease 2019: A Model-Based Analysis'. *The Lancet. Infectious Diseases* 20 (6): 669–77. https://doi.org/10.1016/S1473-3099(20)30243-7.

Voinov, Alexey, and Francois Bousquet. 2010. 'Modelling with Stakeholders'. *Environmental Modelling & Software* 25(11):1268–81.

Weber, Max. 1949. *Max Weber on the Methodology of the Social Sciences*, translated and edited by Edward A. Shils and Henry A. Finch. Glencoe, IL: Free Press.

Weisberg, Michael. 2013. *Simulation and Similarity: Using Models to Understand the World*. New York: Oxford University Press.

Williams, Mary. 2011. 'My Life as a Lab Rat'. *Salon*, 24 November. www.salon.com/2011/11/24/my_life_as_a_lab_rat/.

Winsberg, Eric. 2010. *Science in the Age of Computer Simulation*. Chicago, IL: University of Chicago Press. https://bit.ly/3ZMZdG5.

2012. 'Values and Uncertainties in the Predictions of Global Climate Models'. *Kennedy Institute of Ethics Journal* 22 (2): 111–37.

2018. *Philosophy and Climate Science*. Cambridge: Cambridge University Press.

2022. 'Who Is Responsible for Global Health Inequalities after Covid-19?'. *Global Epidemiology* 4: 100081. https://doi.org/10.1016/j.gloepi.2022.100081.

Winsberg, Eric, and Stephanie Harvard. 2022. 'Purposes and Duties in Scientific Modelling'. *Journal of Epidemiology and Community Health* 76 (5): 512–17.

Xie, Richard Z., Erica deFur Malik, Mark T. Linthicum, and Jennifer L. Bright. 2021. 'Putting Stakeholder Engagement at the Center of Health Economic Modeling for Health Technology Assessment in the United States'. *Pharmacoeconomics* 39 (6): 631–8. https://doi.org/10.1007/s40273-021-01036-3.

Cambridge Elements ☰

Philosophy of Science

Jacob Stegenga
University of Cambridge

Jacob Stegenga is a Reader in the Department of History and Philosophy of Science at the University of Cambridge. He has published widely on fundamental topics in reasoning and rationality and philosophical problems in medicine and biology. Prior to joining Cambridge he taught in the United States and Canada, and he received his PhD from the University of California–San Diego.

About the Series

This series of Elements in Philosophy of Science provides an extensive overview of the themes, topics and debates which constitute the philosophy of science. Distinguished specialists provide an up-to-date summary of the results of current research on their topics, as well as offering their own take on those topics and drawing original conclusions.

Cambridge Elements ≡

Philosophy of Science

Printed in the United States
by Baker & Taylor Publisher Services